CHANGE IT!
Create a Career Centered College Culture

Don Philabaum

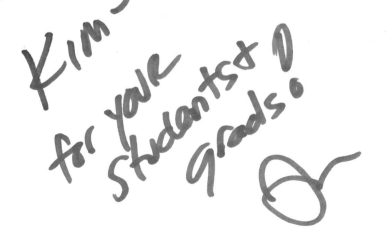

Change It!
Create a Career Centered College Culture

Copyright 2014 © by Donald R. Philabaum

First Printing: January 2014

Managing Editor: Ashley Justice - ashley@justicewebsites.com
Graphic Designer: Daniel Yeager - daniel@nu-images.com
Cartoons: Josey Thomas - tjmalay11@hotmail.com

Career Centered College Culture

a philosophy and process that puts a student's career at the center of every campus activity, event, or course, and is endorsed and supported by parents, students, faculty, administrators, alumni, and business leaders.

FOREWORD

Robert Shindell, Ph.D.

It's time for a change on your college campus!

The current state of how higher education transitions students to life "after college" is showing signs of stress.

Career services practitioners are doing everything in their power to deliver high tech, high touch career services to students. Unfortunately graduates and their parents are expecting more.

And so is the senior leadership of our institutions.

In a time when students need it most, career practitioners on college and university campuses around the country are having to work with more students, more alumni and increasing niche audiences with less resources.

A 2012 survey of nearly 600 career center directors around the country showed me how big a battle they have. Here is what they thought of their grads' career readiness:

- 55.4 percent didn't think grads' resumes were ready to hand out.

- 48.1 percent didn't think grads were ready for their first professional job searches.

- 77.4 percent didn't think students grasped what it takes to get a job.

It's clear the current strategies are not working, but what are we doing differently today to solve this problem?

The obvious is increase funding and staffing so the career center can engage more students and alumni. A more difficult solution would be to require students to take ownership of their career. Another might be to require students to take career courses.

Regardless of the aforementioned changes, each campus has to find their own way to change the paradigm and do something to be a resource to students, grads and alumni.

On many campuses senior administrators do not understand how what you do in career services can have a direct impact on:

- Increased enrollment
- Retention
- Graduation rates
- Contributions from alumni

By shifting this conversation to this strategic level it will help us to position career services as a value-added service provider to our institutions, our students, and our employer partners. The bottom line is that if we continue to do what we have always done, we cannot have the expectation of different results.

It is time for a change. So what can you do?

Read on, Don will share dozens--if not hundreds--of ideas, facts, stats and concepts that will help you lead a discussion on your campus to create a career centered college culture.

Robert Shindell, Ph.D. is the Vice President and Chief Learning Officer for Intern Bridge, Inc, the nation's premier college recruiting and consulting firm. Dr. Shindell has successfully held a variety of professional leadership roles in higher education during his career and is highly regarded as an expert in the area of the transition to the world-of-work for students.

TABLE OF CONTENTS

Foreword   5

Preface   15

Tips   19

The Worst of Times, The Best of Times   21

Grads Are Clueless About How to Find Jobs   29

**Creating a Career Centered College Culture
Is Good For Business**   37

**12 Ways to Integrate Career Management
in Your Culture**   45

Listen to what business leaders have to say   49

Run your Career Center by the numbers!   55

Create alumni programming focused on networking
and building successful careers   59

Build your career center in the "clouds"   63

Immerse students in personal reflection, career
evaluation and self-study   71

Connect students with a minimum of 40 alumni by

graduation day 75

Provide a core career curriculum 79

Integrate career learning opportunities with classes 83

Require students to write career and job search plans 87

Build a career support team for students and grads 93

The employers of your alumni are your new gold mine! 97

Put your career center under a different department 101

Chapter Summary 107

10 Ideas to Shape Your Department's Future 111

Grads need help in the transition from campus
to corporate life 113

Career centers' Future? Charge Fees for Levels of Service 117

Your President Is Going TO LOVE "Shared Services"
for Career Services 121

Career services "in the cloud" accessible by mobile devices 125

Get Parents to Work For Your Career center 129

3 Reasons to Start a Campus Career Club 133

Proven Way to Help More Grads Prepare for Job Search 137

Performance Based Funding
- What Your Career Center Needs to Know! 141

How Do Your Students, Grads & Alumni Rate
Your Career center? 145

Help Alumni Build Successful Careers 149

The Realities Your Grads Face 153

Your Class of 2014 Will Lose $12,000,000 in Wages 155

8 Ways Organizations are "Waging War"
on Students & Grads! 161

Students and Parents put Too Much Focus On
Getting Into College 167

5 Reasons Graduates Do Not Get Jobs!   171

The Quick Death of College Internships as We Know Them   177

New Grad Employability Exam   183

Why Can't Johnny Find a Job?   189

When Will Parents and Students Revolt?   193

What Does Your College Owe Graduates?   197

Research to Build Your Strategies On   **201**

Survey of Career Professionals Suggest Grads'
Resumes ARE NOT Job Search Ready!   203

Employers Are Not Thrilled With The Quality of Your
Grads - Is Your President Listening?   207

Graduates Lack "Soft Skills" Needed in the College
to Corporate Transition   213

McKinsey and Company Report Confirms
- Grads Not Ready for the Marketplace   217

Career center Professionals are– Re-thinking Success   223

Reach Alumni with Scalable Career Services   **231**

Your Alumni Want You to Provide Career Coaching
& Job Placement Services!   233

The Jury Is In! Your Alumni Want Help Networking!   237

3 Ways to Help Alumni Get Jobs   243

Annual Mentoring Campaign!   247

Who Should Be Leading This Change?   **253**

Career center Directors Know How To Fix Grad
Unemployment, But Administrators Are Not Listening!   255

College Requires Community Service
- But NOT Career Study!   259

"An Open Letter to College Presidents",
Is BAD News for Career Services   265

Rutgers University Fired The Wrong Guy!   269

What is your College President FOCUSED on?   273

Your College Does Not Have to Go Out Of Business
Like Newspapers Are   277

Will President Obama Help GRADS Get Jobs?   283

Moving to a "Career Centered" Culture   **287**

Do Careers Get Enough Focus On Your Campus?   289

It Takes a Campus to Build a Successful Career!   293

University of Phoenix Builds College Culture Around
Career Exploration & Management   297

Who Are Your Customers? Students or the Companies
That Hire Them?   301

What are Your Plans to Increase the Number of
Career Center Visits?   305

In Grads' Time of Need, Colleges Cut Career Center Budgets   309

Require - Make - Demand Students Invest
Time In Their Careers   313

It All Starts with Resources   **319**

10 Ways To Get More Resources for Your Career Center   321

Pennywise and Pound Foolish?   **325**

Summary   331

Acknowledgements   334

About the Author   337

This book is dedicated to career center professionals!

Career center professionals are true entrepreneurs.

Not only do they have to convince people to use their services, they have to organize career fairs, develop career curriculums, reach out to faculty, build and maintain relationships with hiring managers, recruiters and business leaders, and coach and advise more students than they should ever be expected to handle - even if they worked 24 hours a day.

Furthermore, they have to do this with a declining budget at a time of increasing expectations from parents, students, government and the media.

It's an impossible task, but from the perspective of both students and the companies that hire them, it's one of the most important responsibilities on campus!

PREFACE

 I've spoken to at least a thousand alumni and career professionals since 1995 about how to use the Internet to increase alumni networking and mentoring, with the goal of helping alumni secure new jobs and do business with one another.

Their ideas and suggestions have become the foundation of nearly a dozen white papers and books.

This book ties it all together by sharing 12 ways your career center, alumni association, faculty, and staff can all work together to develop a culture both on and off campus that is focused on what grads and alumni want –

successful lives and careers!

I've also included nearly 50 mini-chapters based on articles from my blog that share ideas, strategies and solutions to everything from getting students to take ownership of their careers, to acquiring more resources for your career center.

My hope is that you will be able to lead the discussion on your campus to create a career centered college campus.

Your department is the key to your college's survival.

The future of your college's success is not in athletics, not in foreign students, not in palatial residence halls, or even an out of this world health and wellness center. <u>No, the future of your campus lies in *your* department, the Career Center.</u>

Join me in an ongoing discussion about how you can build bridges across campus to create a career centered environment for students.

don@talentmarks.com

"Employed alumni are giving alumni!"

Richard Bolles, Author

TIPS

Here's how to get the most out of this book:

Think of this book as a workbook that you can pick up and use for the areas you are most interested in -- and then skip the rest.

I bet that's not something you hear from many authors!

The chapter you will *not* want to skip is *12 Ways to Create a Career Centered College Culture*. The ideas discussed there will help reinforce what you already know you need to do and give you the data, stats and information to convince management to adopt your long range strategies.

The rest of the book contains mini-chapters that examine issues, ideas and solutions to help you develop a scalable career services strategy that can not only provide analytics to you and your superiors, but more importantly help more students get internships and jobs. Each mini-chapter offer suggestions about how you can implement the strategy. There are more than 150 suggestions and ideas you can use to build your department's career center strategy.

Also, please make it a point to read the conclusion, "Pennywise and Pound Foolish?" where I compare your budget and staffing levels to other departments on campus. This summary will give you powerful formulas you can adapt and share with management.

Finally, visit www.talentmarks.com and sign up for our monthly webinars and discussions revolving around these ideas.

I used to bite my tongue and hold my breath,
Scared to rock the boat and make a mess...
So I sat quietly, agreed politely;
I guess that I forgot I had a choice
I let you push me past the breaking point;
I stood for nothing, so I fell for everything.

I got the eye of the tiger, a fighter, dancing through the fire
'Cause I am a champion and you're gonna hear me roar--
Louder, louder than a lion
'Cause I am a champion and you're gonna hear me roar.

Katy Perry, Roar

THE WORST OF TIMES, THE BEST OF TIMES

For grads, these are truly the worst of times.

I've tracked dozens of surveys and reports over the past couple of years related to grad and alumni employment. There are reports that analyze grad readiness for the job market, surveys by hiring authorities on the quality of the grads colleges prepare, and surveys of career professionals.

During my research I didn't find any report that painted a rosy picture on graduate employment! The research we found shows:

- An increasing number of grads who are unemployed or underemployed

- That employers are disappointed about how colleges are preparing students for their first professional jobs

To anyone working in the career center industry its becoming quite apparent from the steady release of surveys, research and reports, that upper management at colleges across the nation are ignoring them. If colleges and universities were taking these surveys and all the research seriously, the career center would have seen a massive increase in funding and staffing over the past 5 years. But, it hasn't.

In our mutual quest to create a career centered college culture, let's step back and take a moment to listen to what these reports are telling us.

- According to research conducted by the Heldrich Center for Workforce Development at Rutgers University, only 56 percent of the class of 2010 had a job — any job — one year after graduation compared with 90 percent in 2007.

- The Associated Press --with the help of researchers from Northeastern University, Drexell University and the Economic Policy Institute-- reported in 2012 that 53.6 percent of bachelor's degree-holders under the age of 25 were jobless or underemployed.

- A report issued by The Center for College Affordability & Productivity in 2013 provides similar findings. Their report showed nearly 48 percent of employed U.S. college graduates are in jobs that require less than a four-year college education. The report goes on to say about five million college graduates are in jobs that require less than a high-school education.

- The Bureau of Labor Statistics, reported in May, 2013, that college graduates age 20-24 had the highest rate of unemployment in the country with 13.2 percent being unemployed.

What is anyone doing to improve this untenable situation?

These reports are showing that conditions are not only bad, but they will get WORSE!

In the report mentioned above by The Center for College Affordability & Productivity (CCAP), the number of college grads will grow by 19 million between 2010 and 2020, while the number of jobs requiring a college degree is expected to grow by less than 7 million. You do the math. It means 12 million graduates over the next 6 years will be struggling to find jobs that requires the expensive degrees for which they have paid. Assuming that the average grad invested $60,000 in his or her education, that means that 12,000,000 students who are going to college to get a job over the next 8 years will hand over $720,000,000,000 dollars to colleges and end up worse off for their efforts.

If you don't believe this prediction, consider the reality many grads are already living today!

In the CCAP report, Ohio University professor, Professor Richard Vedder, says, "as many as one out of three college graduates today are in jobs that previously or historically have been filled by people with lesser educations, jobs that do not require higher-level learning skills, critical thinking skills, writing skills or anything of that nature." He goes on to cite in the report that, "20 percent of cab drivers have college degrees," and, "300,000 waitresses have college degrees."

The CCAP report dug deeper into historical data looking for past and future employment trends and discovered that total college graduate employment in jobs that did not require a college degree increased from 953,000 in 1967 to 5.06 million individuals in 1990. That is a HUGE number.

There are a whole lot of people who are giving colleges a significant amount of money and not getting a return on their investments. This is a huge public relations problem for your department and your college. Like any consumers, if a ever increasing number of your graduates fail to get a return on their investments they are going to make a whole lot of noise that the college sold them on a promise and never delivered.

With all of this mounting evidence, little is being done to give career centers the resources to bring about the changes necessary to be relevant to their customer bases in these changing, uncertain times.

You know these facts better than most.

You and your colleagues have been struggling to provide more services to more students with ever decreasing resources... and you are not alone.

- The National Association of Colleges and Employers data shows that nationwide the median operating budget for career centers shrank 8 percent between 2010 and 2012 providing career professionals with a meager $31,000 to run their departments

- The same survey completed by over 800 colleges and universities, showed there is an average of one career professional for every 1,645 students. Compare that to colleges that boast a student to faculty ratio of 1:20 students.

This lack of administrative support for the resources and staffing that is needed comes at a price. A study sponsored by the Career Advisory Board found that:

- 55.4 percent didn't think grads' resumes were ready to hand out.

- 48.1 percent didn't think grads were ready for their first professional job searches.

- 77.4 percent didn't think students grasped what it takes to get a job

All of this has a very personal and long lasting effect on graduates and their families.

- Research is showing grads that start their careers during economic downturns will earn 6-8 percent less than their predecessors, and it will take more than a decade to catch up.

- The average grad now has over $27,000 in student loans and nearly $5,000 in credit card debt, which will require a monthly payment of over $370 a month to keep up with minimum payment and interest charges.

- According to The National Association of Colleges and Employers it will take graduates on average 7.4 months to find a job after graduation.

  All of this points to a system that is definitely not meeting the needs of the people it serves. In stronger words, the system is broken.

- How can we feel good about ourselves when college policies are having such a deleterious effect on the careers of students and alumni?

- How can we run a business when more than 50% of our customers are not getting value out of our services?

Who is going to fix it?

The answer is YOU!

You are in a perfect position to be a the agent on your campus that brings about systemic change which will have a far reaching effect on the lives of the students on your campus today, and for generations of students who follow.

When times get bad, good people take action!

While these are truly the worst of times for college graduates, there has NEVER been a better time for you to take action. You have an opportunity to bring about changes that will put an emphasis on career exploration, planning and management. Remember, you are not alone! You have the support of parents, students, legislators, businesses and community leaders! Now you need management support.

But how?

First, continue to join me in exploring the many issues and problems you face and keep an open mind about the ideas and solutions discussed throughout this book.

Second, start asking questions of those to whom you report.

To become a change agent, you have to start by asking the obvious questions and engage everyone you can in finding solutions.

For example, you might start by asking:

- Why can't we help 100 percent of all grads who want a job (and follow our career planning strategies) land a job BEFORE they graduate?

- Why do our grads and alumni have to *stumble* through the job search process if they are going to do it so many times?

- Why can't our college use the power of its alumni, business network and curriculum to help MORE students get internships and jobs?

What really saddens me is that we are continuing to send graduates into a world where according to the Department of Labor they will go through 11-14 job searches by the time they are 38 years old. Our grads need to become masters of the job search process, not neophytes.

How unfortunate!

Imagine the reduced stress graduates and alumni would experience and satisfaction they could gain if they knew how to network, how to build their personal brands, how to use Social Media in their job searches, and how to build keyword-laden resumes.

Studies show the job search process is one of the most stressful periods in an adult's life and ranks right up there with public speaking and dealing with a death in the family. It doesn't have to be that way.

If you don't bring about change, you will still get the blame!

You are in a no-win situation. Research by NACE shows over 60 percent of graduating seniors will either never visit the career center, or will visit only once or twice.

I run into parents, students, and alumni in my travels around the globe and when I tell them what I do, the next statement I invariably hear is, "The career center never did anything for me (or my kid, my neighbor, nephew, etc.)." You might have experienced this too.

The Heldrich report mentioned above found that 58 percent of graduates surveyed did not think the career center did enough to prepare them for their job searches. You and I know that's ridiculous. You know the old adage, "You can lead a horse to water, but you can't make it drink". Likewise it's not your department's fault that students failed to take ownership of their careers. It's not your department's fault that students didn't avail themselves of your services.

This situation is not a reflection on your department and staff, but it is a reflection on the college's lack of commitment to careers and becoming a career centered college campus.

Becoming a career centered college campus offers huge payoffs

Investing in your students' futures offers HUGE payoffs. Every department on campus will benefit. Admissions will have better employment stats to use to increase enrollment, your department will gain more resources, the alumni office will see more alumni networking and engaging in annual giving, and the development department will see more contributions!

You have a unique opportunity to change the culture on your campus and help grads and alumni lead successful careers. Under your watch, you can bring in a fundamental change that will transcend you and your efforts.

Cousin Eddie in the movie Christmas Vacation said it best when the entire family was standing around Clark (who was opening an envelope that had just been delivered). After making an announcement that he was going to use the bonus money in the envelope to put in a family pool, and fly everyone in attendance in for the opening, Clark opened the envelope. As he silently examined the letter in disbelief, Clark's wife, Ellen asked if the bonus check was more than he anticipated.

When Clark read the letter announcing his Christmas bonus was a membership in the Jelly of The Month club, Cousin Eddie said, "Clark that's a gift that keeps on giving the whole year."

You can start a series of changes on your campus that will give grads a gift that keep on giving, a gift they will use dozens of times during critical circumstances in their lives, a gift that keeps on giving.

##

We started this chapter with a quote from Katy Perry's song Roar.

For a little inspiration to help you step forward and lead your campus in a quest to create a career centered college culture, go to YouTube and listen to Katy's song, feel the passion she is sharing and keep thinking about what you want to do to help more students get internships, and grads get jobs. Let it fuel your fire and drive your passion.

Then let your voice roar on your campus!

While this is the worst of times for students who are starting their careers, you can help them compete by giving ALL grads the knowledge, skills and strategies to stand out in a crowded job market.

"To be ignorant of one's ignorance is the malady of the ignorant."
-Amos Bronson Alcott

2 GRADS ARE CLUELESS ABOUT HOW TO FIND JOBS

Man's DNA did not include instructions about how to look for a job!

Hunt for food --yes-- but build a personal brand, learn how to network, create a keyword-laden resume, use social media, or use personal marketing techniques – NO!

Research we've conducted confirms that.

During the TalentMarks annual 12 Hour Virtual Career Marathon which features 24 of the world's top career authors, grads were polled to learn more about their job search skills and strategies.

- Over 60 percent were spending only 1-5 hours per WEEK on their job searches.

- 95 percent did not have a career or job search plan.

- Over 30 percent had never connected with an alum and 60 percent had networked with only one alum during the entire college experience.

- The principle strategy grads used to get a job was to post their resumes on job boards.

The first stat shocked me.

How can graduates expect to get a job when they invest virtually no time or effort into looking for a job?

The last fact saddened me.

I worried because grads didn't know any better and they spent their time posting their resumes on job boards. The practice of posting resumes on job boards is generally a huge waste of time. Research has shown the average person searching for a job will spend more than 40 hours a month on job boards, yet less than 12 percent of all jobs that are eventually accepted result from a random posting on a job board. When there are so many other proven ways to look for a job, graduates are spending the most time on the least productive activity.

Let's look at it from this perspective:

Studies show the average hiring manager receives more than 250 resumes for a job and spends less than 30 seconds reviewing them. Price Waterhouse, for example, received over 250,000 resumes on their corporate website in one year and hired less than 1 percent of the applicants.

Think about that for a moment.

That means 247,500 people invested time to find the opportunity, personalize their resume for the positions Price Waterhouse had, and do follow-up calls, emails and letters. This group of job seekers probably wasted a half a million hours just applying for positions at Price Waterhouse. I feel bad for the hiring manager who has to find a logical way to decipher all of the information being thrown at him or her, I really feel bad for the candidates who are spinning their wheels and wasting their time when they need to be working and supporting their families.

These facts and stats along with daily discussions with career professionals gave me a clear understanding about how totally clueless grads are when it comes to looking for a job. It eventually led me to write the book, , <u>The Unemployed Grad and What Parents Can Do About It</u> for the general public, and an edited version, <u>The Employed Grad, Knowledge, Skills & Strategies Your Grad Will Need to Get a Job</u> that colleges can distribute to parents.

This generation, more so then previous generations, is clueless when it comes to searching for a job--, not because they are not as smart-- but because the employment landscape and process is so different today. For most of the parents of Millennials, the job search process started with a simple resume, the classified ads, telephone calls from a land-based phone, and then sending resumes in the mail.

Today, not only is the job search process more competitive for grads, but there are many different skills, knowledge and strategies grads need to master in order to even make it to the interview. To take ownership of one's career today students should invest time to:

1. Explore their personality, behaviors, and interests via assessments.

2. Explore careers, industries and jobs that are right for him or her.

3. Build keyword-laden resumes.

4. Create a job search strategy.

5. Learn how to network professionally.

6. Use Linked In, Twitter, Facebook and other Social Media outlets to sniff out job leads.

7. Obtain and "nail" interviews, and then professionally follow up.

8. Build a personal brands by creating professional blogs and Twitter accounts.

9. Learn how to transition from campus to the corporate world.

10. Pick up communications, teamwork, leadership, ethics and other skills that business leaders routinely say students are lacking.

Students can't master even one of these with one or two visits to the career center their senior year.

Unfortunately, for the vast majority of students - their career strategy is to "wing it."

Most students assume they can send out a resume, get a phone call and step into their own office and a $50k job. You know it doesn't work that way and you face the challenge of trying to educate them about the realities of getting a job. Who can do that two weeks from graduation?

Students would be wise to take the advice of Richard Bolles author of *"What Color is Your Parachute?"* Among the 10 Truths of Job Hunting, Bolles number 2 Truth says:

> "Mastering the job-hunt this time, and for the rest of your life, is a lot of hard work and takes some hard thinking. The more you work and the more thinking you put into pursuing your job-hunt, and doing homework on yourself, the more successful your job-hunt is likely to be. Caution: Are you lazy, day by day? Uh, oh! Most people do their job-hunts or career changes the same way they do life."

As you know, looking for a job is a full time job.

Tony Beshara is President of one of Texas's largest employment placement firms and has put over 8,000 people in jobs in the last 30 years. Tony knows what it takes to get a job. In fact, he will frequently rattle off statistics that would make any student cringe:

- It takes 100 phone calls to reach 10 hiring managers of which only 2 may have jobs.

- It will take the average person 16 interviews to get a job.

Tony has also written 3 career books and has become the resident career expert on Dr. Phil's TV program. Tony confirms the belief that students are not ready for their first professional job searches.

> "No one is born with job search skills. Today there are multiple channels and new Social Media tools that increase the complexity of searching for a job. Students need more training about where to spend their job search time and the fundamentals of how to search for a job. This isn't just my opinion it's the feedback I get daily from hiring managers."

There are jobs out there!

I know in the first chapter I spent a good deal of time focusing on the doom and gloom aspect of this situation, but there are jobs out there grads and alumni can get. They have a better shot then most, but they need to know how to get them.

While there are more people looking for jobs then jobs are available, the "Help Wanted" Signs are still being hung in every corner of our nation. David Perry, author of *Guerilla Marketing for Job Search 3.0* shared this information with the 700 career centers participating in our Grad Career Webinar series:

In the six months from May 2011 to October 2011, companies/ organizations hired 24,469,000 people. That comes out to:

- 4,078,166 per month
- 134,938 per day
- 5,664 per hour
- 94 per minute
- 1.5 per second

At the same time, nearly 3,000,000 jobs went unfilled each month!

With limited resources, the career center has not had the opportunity to invest enough time in graduates who need more coaching and training. As a result they interview poorly, and make the college and all subsequent grads look bad.

One of the reasons graduates are not getting hired is because they lack the soft skills that employers say they need to successfully transition from their campus dorms to their corporate cubicals. Many complain graduates don't have:

- Written communication skills
- Interpersonal skills
- Problem solving skills
- Technical skills
- Teamwork skills

Colleges and Universities that recognize this and ramp up their investments in their career centers will not only give their graduates an edge over graduates from competing colleges, but they will help them build successful career and job search strategies.

Getting ahead of this issue will help admissions recruit more students, help your president improve retention, and improve the the graduation rate. It's worth the time and effort to create a career centered college culture.

You have an opportunity to raise the discussion to another level, to make sure the president's cabinet is aware of the stats, facts and ==more importantly== the individual hardships and effects this lack of focus has on your students, grads and alumni. You need to make sure that your management is aware that your students are looking for jobs that will lead to successful careers. Not just any job will do! This generation is looking for "gainful employment" that is relevant to their major and one that will provide them income streams to live the American dream, as well as pay back their student loans.

Your college owes them this opportunity.

##

I just love Amos Bronson Alcott's quote at the beginning of this chapter.

Not only are students ignorant of what they don't know to get a job and are guilty of not taking ownership of their careers, but in light of ALL of the mounting research and data, management is sadly ignorant of the enormous cost this situation creates for students, grads, and the reputation of the college.

To rectify this situation colleges and universities will need to change their cultures and curriculums and require students to create written career and job search plans.

"No people come into possession of a culture without having paid a heavy price for it."

-James A. Baldwin

3 CREATING A CAREER CENTERED COLLEGE CULTURE IS GOOD FOR BUSINESS

WHY?

1. ENROLLMENT
2. GRADUATE RATES
3. CONTRIBUTIONS
4. LEGISLATION
5. COMPETITION
6. REPUTATION
7. RIGHT THING

Colleges and universities were founded on the premise that their roles were to create responsible, enlightened, and productive citizens that will give back to their communities and nation.

In the "Leave it to Beaver" era and the hundred years prior, that not only made sense, but it worked! Colleges produced enlightened citizens that helped shape our government, institutions and our religious organizations.

College graduates led institutions and organizations using the knowledge they gained during college and expanded the U.S. economy from $1 trillion dollars in the early 70's to over $15 trillion dollars today.

College graduates have also made significant contributions to human rights and health issues and supported worldwide democracy that has literally changed the direction of our planet and species!

It's a phenomenal accomplishment in the history of mankind!

Yet, times have changed!

People, culture, technology, the work environment, jobs, and our habits and behaviors have all changed. We live in a different world totally unrelated to the one in which the career center was originally conceived.

It's time to reboot!

Yes, it's time to change the way we do business in higher education to focus on what customers want and deliver on it. It's time to do whatever it takes, to put whatever resources are necessary into giving the people who are entrusting their life savings and futures what they want: fulfilling careers. It's time to listen to hiring managers and business leaders and do whatever we can, whatever it takes-- even if it's changing or modifying the curricula-- in order to deliver graduates who are fully functional and ready to work on day one.

It's time to listen to you!

This can only happen if you lead the charge.

The goal of this book is to present a dizzying array of ideas, suggestions and strategies that will help you start a conversation on your campus that will lead to creating a career centered college culture.

We define a **career centered college culture** as:

> a philosophy and process that puts a student's career at the center of every campus activity, event, or course and, one that is endorsed and supported by parents, students, faculty, administrators, alumni and business leaders.

This means everyone on campus needs to look at their department to see how they can support the number one goal for students – to prepare for and launch successful careers. The only way to achieve that is to get *everyone*-- faculty, students, staff, parents and even alumni-- behind a plan to focus on helping students build written career and job search plans.

This approach will not fundamentally change the curriculums presented by faculty. If done properly, faculty will find ways to introduce and challenge students to interpret what they are learning in class on how it will benefit those companies or organizations for whom they will eventually work.

It will require a slight modification in the college vision, mission and goals to incorporate not only the development of responsible citizens, but to also give them the skills and knowledge to lead successful careers.

Why should your college do this?

You should do if for a variety of reasons-- not only to help your grads and alumni have successful careers-- but because there are political and competitive risks that you face if you don't move in this direction. Besides helping your graduates and alumni lead more successful lives, here are seven reasons this focus will benefit your college:

1. It will increase enrollment.

2. It will increase retention and graduation rates.

3. It will increase contributions.

4. It will stay ahead of legislation.

5. It will help your institution stay competitive.

6. Your reputation is at stake.

7. It's the right thing to do.

It will increase enrollment.

The UCLA's Higher Education Research Institute (HERI) reported their annual American Freshman survey is showing an ever-increasing number of students who indicate they are going to college to improve their job prospects. The 2013 survey showed that 88 percent cited, "Getting a better job" as a "VERY important reason to pursue a college education."

Imagine the positive response your admissions team will have when they share with prospective students and their parents your college has a career centered campus!

Sure, the health and wellness center, complete with a climbing wall, will be important to share with students, as will the newness of your residence halls and student amenities, but more and more prospective students and parents will be weighing decisions on the stats, facts and data about your grad employment rate and how your career centered college campus has made a difference.

It will increase retention and graduation rates.

Every college is throwing time, money and resources at trying to improve both retention and the graduation rate. Based on the HERI survey mentioned above, wouldn't it make sense to keep students focused on their careers?

It will increase contributions.

If the value of the diploma continues to diminish and the satisfaction of a record number of new graduates continues to decrease, the college could face decades of declining contributions.

I was talking to Gerry Crispen, co-founder of CareerXroads, who holds regular meetings with the top human resources people in the country, and he shared with me a personal story about this. Gerry was attending a speaker's presentation 35 years ago, where a little known theologian who had written a new book, *What Color is Your Parachute?*, suggested that, "Employed alumni are giving alumni!"

Is your college doing everything in its power to help advance the careers of not only your grads, but your alumni? Are you putting their personal and business success before your requests for donations? You know the phrase, "you have to give before you ask." If you invest MORE in their careers, I guarantee they will have more to share with you over their lifetimes. By taking this step, you will not have to beg for money; alumni will gladly give back.

It will comply with legislation.

With the total value of student loan debt tipping the 1 TRILLION mark and outstripping the total credit card debt of ALL consumers, Congress is starting to focus on the cost of education, and the students'/alumni's return on investment. They have already put for-profits under their thumbs and have passed legislation requiring them to share data with the government that their degrees are providing "gainful employment" to graduates. If they can't, they risk losing access to the student loan system.

The Federal government provides over $30 billion dollars in loans and grants each year and another $30 billion in research grants to colleges. Now that they are "holding the "bag for a trillion dollars of student loans, and their constituents are beating them up with stories about the inability to get jobs and pay back their student loans, they are listening.

The Dodd-Frank law requires the Education Department and the new Consumer Financial Protection Bureau to report on private education loans by July 2012. As part of that, the Consumer Bureau recently announced it was seeking answers from students, schools and lenders to a series of questions. You should anticipate that the student loan process will undergo a whole new set of rules, regulations, qualifications which will affect all schools, majors, subjects and students alike. The results have the potential to fundamentally require colleges to reinvent how they do business.

The "gainful employment" legislation is a first notice to all colleges to begin making changes in the way they market, operate and serve their customers.   All colleges should carefully read the requirements posted in this bill that, although it has a slow fuse, is already changing recruiting behaviors.

Colleges and universities who step up to the plate and center their college educations around making sure graduates have successful careers will be ahead of future legislative changes and public relation issues.

It will help your institution stay competitive.

A 2010 report by the Sloan Consortium showed the percentage of students taking online courses was surging. 2009 saw a record 17 percent increase on top of the previous year which held a 12 percent increase.

That was contrasted by only a 1.2 percent growth rate of the overall higher-education student population.

The behaviors of consumers are changing fast and the internet continues to cause the disintermediation of industries. It started with the annihilation of something called the *Encyclopedia Britannica*, stormed through the travel, entertainment, music industries, and it's literally blowing the printed book industry apart.

SmartPhones have become the fasted adopted "appliances" in the history of electronics and they, along with SmartPads, are opening up new behaviors and marketing/engagement channels for students and alumni.

New online education models are developing that are cheaper and more flexible and yet provide a degree that the business world seems to accept.

Organizations that do not adapt to these changes may find themselves modifying some of their college dorms and buildings to retirement communities.

Your reputation is at stake.

Each year you are sending hundreds if not thousands of ambassadors into the business world. Each has the potential to make a positive mark on the institutions for which they work, but at the same they could affect the reputation of your college poorly.

Few administrators have thought through the negative effects of sending a graduate out with so little career training.

- If they have not taken the time to prepare professional resumes, it not only reflects poorly on the graduates, but also on the college.

- If they don't know how to interview and have poor communication skills, it not only reflects poorly on them, but the college and every graduate that follows.

- If it takes 7.4 months or longer to get a job, it reflects poorly on your college and students' and graduates' satisfaction levels plummet!

All of this affects hiring, admissions and contributions! In hindsight, this is probably the number one reason your college should be moving in this direction.

It's the right thing to do!

We mentioned a startling statistic discovered by a NACE Research report, which indicated the average 2011 grad took 7.4 months to get a job.

Your grads and their parents have invested their trust and their families' wealth in your college. The average grad today is spending over $80,000 or more on a four year college degree.

We've got to find a way to help them not only to get internships but to get jobs by the time they graduate.

Assuming the average graduate is earning $3,500 per month or $21 per hour, reducing the college to job cycle by 3 months would be worth over $10,000 to each graduate.

Now that is a graduation present every graduate would thank you for!

If you do nothing, you are sending a powerful message and one that will come back to affect enrollment, pride and contributions. You know the need to do something is great. You know the timing is right. You know the overall effect is vast.

So what are you waiting for?

Your goal of creating a career centered college culture has the potential to be powerful and long lasting and dramatically improve the lives of your graduates, as well as the reputation and financial health of your college.

##

James A. Baldwin's quote at the beginning of this chapter reminds us that culture change doesn't happen without a heavy price. To move your campus in this direction it will require you to step on your soap box and shout out to every department, manager and administrator why creating a career centered college campus is the right thing to do for not only the students but for the health of the college too!

Politicians are recognizing JOBS are the number one priority for their constituents. It's the same for your alumni!

"Change will not come if we wait for some other person, or if we wait for some other time. We are the ones we've been waiting for. We are the change that we seek."

-Barack Obama

4 12 WAYS TO INTEGRATE CAREER MANAGEMENT IN YOUR CULTURE

*It's time to put the career center at the center
of a student's education*

So enough moaning and complaining about the realities we face today!

Let's move beyond all that and start looking at ways we can reboot. Let's start looking at how we can create a more measurable, repeatable and predictable career center plan.

We'll do that by examining the following strategies:

1. Listening to what business leaders have to say

2. Running the career center by the numbers

3. Focusing on helping your alumni during transitions in their lives

4. Building a career center in the "clouds"

5. Personal reflection, career evaluation, and self-study

6. Connecting students with a minimum of 40 alumni by graduation day

7. Providing a core career curriculum

8. Integrating career learning opportunities with classes

9. Requiring students to write career and job search plans

10. Building a career support team for students.

11. Understanding that the employers of your alumni are your new gold mine!

12. Placing the career center under a different department

These ideas will provide you the facts, stats, solutions and strategies to help you create a career centered college culture. Each will revolve around building a new model, creating new partnerships and adopting proven, relevant strategies for these uncertain times.

Along the way, we'll challenge you to set some new goals and to get support on your campus. The number one issue we encourage you to take on is to *increase the number of grads who get jobs by the time they graduate.* With research suggesting it takes the average grad 7.4 months to get a job, what if you were able to help them find jobs in 4 months? Each month that your students beat the national average, your graduates will put $3,000 to $5,000 of salary into their pockets.

Imagine if you were able to help 100 of your grads cut four months each off their job searches: That would result in $1,200,000 to $2,000,000 in salary for them as a combined group. Each grad would have an extra $12,000 - $20,000 to use to pay down their college loans.

Ready?

Let's change the culture on your campus!

As President Barack Obama's quote suggests you are the change you've been waiting for. Someone on your campus has to make the first move to help your college focus on outcomes and help your graduates and alumni have successful careers. You have the experience, you have the knowledge, and you are closest to the situation, so let your voice roar!

"You can't fake listening. It shows."

-Raquel Welch

LISTEN TO WHAT BUSINESS LEADERS HAVE TO SAY!

In a previous business I founded, we photographed 200,000 college graduates as the president awarded each of them their diplomas.

I always got the feeling from attending literally a thousand graduation ceremonies over two decades that colleges and universities considered their jobs done on graduation day. As the chairs were folded and the banners were taken down, the staff and faculty started to think about the next class and any responsibility to the current class quickly faded.

The longer I work in higher education, the more I look at graduation day as a transitional day for the college. It's a day in which the college stops focusing on helping students acquire the knowledge to graduate and begins helping them apply the knowledge they have acquired.

It got me thinking. Does anyone at the college:

- Survey hiring managers to find out what they can do to better prepare graduates so their graduates can immediately step in and be productive employees?

- Talk with business leaders to see if their graduates have the skill sets needed to lead those companies?

I couldn't find individual colleges that conducted these types of surveys and acted on them, but I did find an association who polled more than 1,000 hiring managers.

The American Association of College Accreditation, the nonprofit organization that provides accreditation to over 800 colleges, engaged FTI Consulting to conduct a survey of hiring decision-makers in order to learn how college grad job applicants are perceived with regards to the knowledge and skills graduates need to succeed in the workplace.

The results published in November 2011 showed the industry thinks higher education could be doing a better job preparing graduates for the workplace:

1. Only 7% believe the higher education system does an "excellent" job preparing students, while 54% say it does a "good" job and 39% say "only fair" or "poor."

2. 45% of decision-makers believe that most students would be better served by an education that specifically prepares them for the workplace. 55% prefer a broad-based education that helps them choose their best career paths.

3. Hiring decision-makers admit to difficulties in finding the right applicants to fill open positions.

4. Only 16% say that applicants are "very prepared" with the knowledge and skills they need for the job. 63% say applicants are "somewhat prepared" and another 21% say applicants are unprepared.

5. 54% of hiring decision-makers report that the process of finding applicants with the necessary skills and knowledge sets is difficult.

6. 29% of decision-makers say that finding the right applicant has become more difficult over the past few years. Only 15% say it has become easier.

The full report is an interesting read and is available on the American Association of College Accreditation's website. It should be a must-read for everyone on the president's council, the board of trustees, and faculty. I've not seen a report in a long time that is saying as strongly as this report suggests that business professionals are looking for improvements in the "products" they are being offered.

After reading the report it might make sense to:

1. Conduct a gap analysis and evaluate where your students are not matching business professionals' expectations.

2. Build new curriculums and programs to offset the knowledge and skills shortage.

3. Better prepare your graduates for the campus to corporate transition and offer more training in the skill areas business leaders suggest students are lacking.

4. Make it easier for business professionals to be able to find and hire your graduates.

If you can accomplish any one of these, but hopefully all four, you will be positioning your graduates to not only stand out in a crowded job market and get more interviews, but to go on to have more successful careers, with less stress and effort when transitioning from job to job. More importantly, this will help students get jobs, because businesses that know you are listening to them and acting on their suggestions will look at more of your students' resumes, interview them more often, and offer them jobs at higher wages.

It really wouldn't be that hard to implement a program to determine business satisfaction. All you need are a couple of good student interns and the ability to contact last year's grads and find out which companies now employ them. Your interns can track down grads via their Facebook accounts, the alumni online directory, or your own lists and ask the contacts for the names of their supervisors. With that information in hand, you not only have new business contacts to add to your list, but you can send out a nice letter with a few survey questions asking how prepared these graduates have proven themselves, and if the supervisors would consider other graduates from your college. Consider inviting them to a webinar or campus discussion or asking their advice about what they would like the college to do to better prepare future hires.

There are a limited number of colleges who are taking these next steps and acting on such information. Here is an example of a **student salary money back guarantee** offered to employers of MTI College students:

We at MTI are acutely aware of the time and energy that employers invest in new employees. We have made it our mission to prepare our students to be reliable assets in their chosen fields of study. MTI's confidence in our graduates now comes with a spectacular salary-back guarantee! MTI College is pleased to introduce the MTI Guaranteed Graduate program that allows employers to hire MTI graduates with the confidence of knowing that their new employees have the backing of the college that prepared them for the job.

Talk about listening to customers and acting on their feedback! This one is pretty phenomenal.

I know you are thinking that you will be retired before this idea gets adopted at your college, but you never know. There is a perfect storm heading your direction brought on by competition online, the economy, changing consumer behaviors, technology and the government. This perfect storm will force every department in your college to align around common objectives to survive!

Don't believe me? Listen to what Peter Drucker has to say about the future of higher education:

> "Thirty years from now the big university campuses will be relics. Universities won't survive. It's as large a change as when we first got the printed book. Do you realize that the cost of higher education has risen as fast as the cost of health care? And for the middle-class family, college education for their children is as much of a necessity as is medical care—without it the kids have no future. Such totally uncontrollable expenditures, without any visible improvement in either the content or the quality of education, means that the system is rapidly becoming untenable. Higher education is in deep crisis."

Or, listen to another Peter, this one - Peter McPherson, a former commercial banker who was president of Michigan State University from 1993 to 2004:

> "Market pressure is going to force educators to think about things unconventionally; every sector of business that has gone through this struggle and has always said 'we can't do it.' That's what health care said, that's what the automobile companies said. But the markets do work, and change does come."

Both Peters' quotes are from 1997.

That was long before the dot com bust, 911, the housing bust, the stock market crash in 2008 and the continual rise in the cost of education. These men knew change would happen long before the forces of the

Internet changed the music, entertainment, news and other industries. It's destined to change your business model as well.

If your campus is focused on your customers' satisfaction and you are doing everything you can to help get them get jobs, and do business with each other-- and you are showing your customers the VALUE you add-- you will improve the odds that you will maintain your market position and your price advantage over the forces working against your industry.

##

I love the Raquel Welsh quote as it reminds me that we can no longer offer lip service to our customers.

We need to be actively-- no, passionately-- listening to the businesses and organizations that hire our graduates to find out what they are thinking – and then act on their thoughts and suggestions! Every professor, staff member, and administrator has a responsibility to the graduates even after they receive their diplomas on graduation day.

You have to decide who your customers are. The businesses that hire your students will likely say that they are YOUR customers and they want to be heard!

"Statistics suggest that when customers complain, business owners and managers ought to get excited about it. The complaining customer represents a huge opportunity for more business."

-Zig Ziglar

RUN YOUR CAREER CENTER BY THE NUMBERS!

Every successful business has to look at their revenue, customer satisfaction, costs and other stats in order to keep on top of their games. The best companies are:

- Continually making tweaks and modifications to their procedures in order to stay competitive.

- Holding departments and people accountable to improve their stats.

...and, if they don't - there are consequences!

If you were the president of a private or public corporation, association and or government agency and 50 percent of your customers were not getting the value they expected out of your product or services, what do you think would happen to you?

- If you were lucky, you'd be given an opportunity to improve the situation.

- If you were not, you'd probably be fired!

By what stats do you manage your career center? Are you tracking:

1. The number of students visiting the career center?

2. The number of students who have written career and job search plans?

3. The number of students who have internships?

4. How long it takes on average for your students to get jobs?

5. How many alumni mentors a student has had by graduation day?

6. The number of years it takes to complete a 4-year degree?

If you are, are you using the data to initiate change or improve your program? The data you collect can become a powerful tool to get more resources for your career center to get AND keep students focused on their careers and job search strategies.

The key is to select 2-3 stats that can drive continual improvement in your organization. If I handed you a page that included the above 6 stats, what would you do with them? Most managers traditionally ask for a quick comparison to the previous year. After that, the stats and the report will be quickly forgotten.

You need to pick a stat that you can:

1. Use to create strategies to improve each year

2. Is easy to explain

3. Tells a story

4. Becomes part of your culture

For example, if you focused on how long it takes the average grad to get a job after graduation, you can show graduates what it will cost them each month by not having a job and then have the story told by peers – who have been there, done that!

According to NACE Research, the average 2011 grad took 7.4 months to get a job. You can tell a story of a grad who worked on his or her career plan and job search strategy and had a job by graduation day and contrast that with a grad that took the full 7.4 months to get a job.

When a student does the math and realizes not having a job by the time he or she graduates will cost between $24,000 and $32,000 in lost wages, (assuming their salary was $3,000 - $4,000 per month), plus the hassles of living at home, issues with paying loans, and not getting on with their lives, chances are he or she will become motivated to invest the time to explore career options, and build a job search strategy.

It's a story that parents and grads need to hear at orientation if you want to get mileage out of it.

Make stats part of your culture

If you made stats part of your culture, everyone in your organization would be responsible to help reach or beat the goals each year.

Consider creating posters and running ads in student publications --all focusing on your numbers. Keep the ads simple. Just publish the numbers and get them thinking about what those numbers means!

The idea is to get everyone, your faculty, staff, alumni and students thinking about it, talking about it and *acting on it.*

You are fighting to get their attention and having a simple number in front of them would not only increase awareness, but buy-in. It's commonly known that it takes 5-6 views before one becomes aware of an ad. You have to use guerilla marketing techniques to get your message out there and use stories to build them into your culture.

This is probably one of the most important steps you will take to move your organization to become focused on becoming a career centered college culture and curriculum organization.

##

Zig Ziglar reminds us that we need to embrace stats as a way to judge customer satisfaction with the value of your products and services. Running your career center by the numbers will put you on a path of continual improvement that will force the entire campus community to get engaged and take ownership.

You have a fantastic opportunity to get more resources for your career center when you collect, analyze and present data to management to justify program improvements and resource requests.

"The richest people in the world look for and build networks, everyone else looks for work."

Robert Kiyosaki

CREATE ALUMNI PROGRAMMING FOCUSED ON NETWORKING AND BUILDING SUCCESSFUL CAREERS

Another way you can help your college change the culture on campus to focus on careers is to encourage your alumni association to help alumni network with one another, and give them the skills and information they need to lead successful careers.

Done properly this will increase mentoring and internships, and increase the likelihood that your students will be hired by alumni!

A research report commissioned by the American Insurance Administrators and the NEATrust, titled, "Current and Desired Relationship with Your Undergraduate Alma Mater" showed that in order to increase contributions and engagement, the alumni association had to give something of value to alumni.

Using the patented interview and interpretation technique known as the Zaltman Metaphor Elicitation Technique, the researchers found that alumni felt as though their alma maters were:

- Treating them like numbers, not people.

- Always asking for something but never giving any value to them.

The report discovered that alumni were looking to the college to continue to provide the education, advice and resources they had as undergrads.

The research suggested, "Universities must show that they have their alum's best interests at heart." The research also suggested that alumni were looking to their alma maters for help in getting jobs, doing business, and in financial matters like buying a home or car or even retiring. <u>What they were not interested in was "8 ways to give back to the college."</u>

Provide career exploration, management and job search programming

The report went on to show that alumni looked to the alumni association as a trusted source of information. They originally put their faith in the college to deliver an education that would provide them with ways to support themselves and the study suggests the alumni association could build on that trust by providing value added services to alumni.

There are a number of ways you could provide scalable career programming to alumni. You are already probably holding events that feature a main speaker. Consider offering a webinar series that focuses on:

1. Job search strategies.

2. Work place issues

3. Soft Skills

There are many benefits of focusing more on networking and helping alumni have successful careers:

1. More alumni will become engaged in student recruitment and mentoring.

2. More successful alumni will contribute – more, and more frequently.

3. You will build relationships with the companies at which alumni are working.

4. Alumni will come back to your college (physically or virtually) for the skills and knowledge needed in our new economy.

It doesn't take a rocket scientist or surveys from Harvard professors to get inside of alumni's minds and find out what they want from the alumni association.

Just ask your graduating seniors!

##

Robert Kiyosaki's quote reminds us in the quote above of the importance of focusing on building a professional network. You can unleash the most powerful network the world has ever seen to help your alumni build successful careers. Examine the programs and strategies you are currently implementing and drop 10 percent of them so you can focus on more events that help your alumni network.

Your alumni are the jet fuel in your "jobs producing" strategy. When you help your alumni lead successful lives, they will help you 10 times more!

"I don't believe that the public knows what it wants; this is the conclusion that I have drawn from my career."

-Charlie Chaplin

BUILD YOUR CAREER CENTER IN THE "CLOUDS"

The career center, at most colleges does not have prime real estate.

Many have been assigned left-over space, or the only space left after all academic, clubs and athletic departments got their spaces.

Some career professionals I've spoken to joke that they were lucky to get the last space left – a converted boiler room! Others have space on the edge of campus, off the beaten path of students' daily treks. Nearly all are dealing with a small space that tends to be open, and not organized for private conversations and/or conference discussions.

Welcome to the offices of the majority of career professionals!

It is a bit surprising that with beautiful new health and wellness centers being built on campuses around the country, career centers are <u>still</u> <u>dealing with the smallest per square foot space even though they have</u> <u>the responsibility to serve every student on campus and the occasional</u> <u>alum who stops by.</u>

Some would say that might be why, on a nationwide basis, only 30% of the students that graduate visit the career center office.

If you agree with some of the strategies we've shared and are interested in requiring all of your students to take personal ownership of their career plans, while at the same time completing an organized, well-thought out curriculum, <u>you are going to need more space to accommodate</u> <u>serving all students, freshman through seniors.</u>

With today's economy and budget cuts, that is not likely to happen. The only logical way to accommodate this strategy is to move your new career services to "the clouds!"

The timing to do that could not be better, for three reasons:

1. Nearly every college has introduced a series of online e-learning strategies and courses designed to allow students to watch videos of classes, submit papers, discuss class assignments and even take tests online. You already have systems and procedures that are driving students to interact via the internet.

2. Today's Millennials' behavior is being changed by the powerful SmartPhones, SmartPads and video communication tools available today. They are spending a greater amount of their time accessing the information they want 24/7. Research is suggesting students prefer getting their news, information and entertainment this way.

3. Students have busy schedules. With classes, assignments, tests, reports, group projects, library use and research time, not to mention sports, and club meetings, they just don't have a lot of spare time. Fitting in a visit to the career center is getting more difficult to do. Giving them the option of gaining access to your career center 24/7 will likely increase their participation and career learning.

Margie Decker, Director of Career Services for Strayer University, is responsible for delivering career services to the institution's 90 campuses and their 50,000 students. Margie has been working on techniques to deliver "in the cloud" career services that students can access anytime, anywhere and from any device. According to Margie:

> "We have to be delivering relevant, timely and proven career strategies to students and alumni that match their behaviors. The career center is no longer a destination but more a state of mind. Career services has to be available on demand, yet include personal, one-on-one connections whenever possible."

While the rest of the campus, including academic advising, is moving to online solutions, the career center is not being afforded technological solutions that would enable them to work smarter, not harder, and serve more students more efficiently.

With a modest increase in resources your career center could be adopting proven, yet innovative technologies and solutions like:

1. An e-learning platform that provides online courses on resume development, interviewing, job searches, using social media, and more

2. Online group coaching using webcam and online discussion tools

3. Webinars to deliver timely and relevant information

4. Social media strategies that enable students to promote the courses and tools to their friends.

5. Online chat agents available 24/7 to answer students questions

6. Smart bulletin boards that encourage crowd source participation

7. Facebook applications to connect alumni and students and to increase internship and job placement

8. Advanced uses of Facebook fan pages to build connections between hiring managers at businesses and students

9. CRM tools that capture students "career plans" and give coaches, mentors, parents and advisors updates of students' progress

10. Online rewards systems to continue to provide recognition for participation, increasing use by rewarding participants

You can use your "in the cloud" strategy to:

- Reach more students and alumni.

- Increase students' job search and interviewing skills.

- Decrease the time you spend on emails, phone calls and common questions.

- Reach more businesses to connect with your students.

Finally, by building a more comprehensive online career strategy and integrating it with your existing services you will be able to:

1. Encourage your students to take more ownership of their career strategies.

2. Focus more on coaching students and less on teaching them.

3. Use social media to let students "encourage" their classmates to develop career strategies.

4. Measure everything automatically.

These final points are important enough that I'd like to take a moment to clarify what we are suggesting.

Encourage your students to take ownership of their career strategies:

By building career strategies "in the clouds," you will be able to provide more variety, content and information to your students at any time. You can also build in customer relationship management (CRM) tools to remind them of opportunities they have overlooked, recognize them for their participation, and encourage them to continue their self-studies.

Some say this generation has been spoon fed for most of their lives. Your goal should be to spark their interests and help them see that the "end game" of employment is in sight so they can actively own and manage their career strategies.

Reduce the mundane and provide more quality one-on-one:

Let's face it. Much of career counseling is repeating the same thing over and over and over to a new audience each day, and each year. Much of it involves basic training. Think for a moment how much of your day you would get back if you didn't have to repeat the same information over and over. Then, think about how much more coaching you could do with students to help them craft a successful career and job search strategy if you did not have to teach each student the fundamentals.

For example:

If you required your students to take an online resume course like those designed by TalentMarks, students would learn about the foundations of a resume, the architecture of a resume, and how to make resumes work for them, and you would be able to start at a whole different level-- helping them build more powerful resumes and reinforcing the information they picked up by viewing the course.

If you used some of the online tools like CareerChat that TalentMarks offers, you would be able to handle incoming questions from your students 24/7 without adding an additional staff person, and you'd also reduce the number of emails and phone calls you'd have to answer.

The career center of the future will learn how to successfully blend off-line and online services in order to serve more – and more effectively – with less time and effort.

Use Social Media to let students "encourage" their classmates to develop their career strategies:

Your online strategy will enable you to take advantage of the powerful viral effects social media tools like Facebook, Twitter and even LinkedIn provide. A smart strategy would enable students that participated in an online resume, job search or networking course to share it with their friends at any time of the day or night. As students see their peers moving forward with their career strategies, peer pressure will help drive participation and enthusiasm.

Measure everything automatically:

The great thing about the internet is everything is automatically measurable.

We foresee a time in the not too distant future where a college will have to show its students are acquiring "gainful employment" in order to pay back their student loans.

Colleges and universities that are requiring students to learn how to look for jobs and build their career strategies will have data they can use to show accreditation firms, *US News and World Report*, and even government agencies. This information can be sorted to show the results of students who have taken ownership of their careers and availed themselves of the career development services vs. those who have not.

By gathering this data, we suspect that a college will have the ability to advertise and market the results from those students who are engaged in their careers and eliminate or not include the stats of students who are not taking ownership of their careers.

Your "in the cloud" strategy will also help you reduce costs. As your demand for services increases, you will be able to scale your services without adding full time equivalents.

Charlie Chaplin reminds us that the public doesn't always know what it wants, until it sees what it wants and then it wants it right away. I can guarantee you that once students experience having access to the services they need, 24/7 through any device, they will wonder why you didn't provide this before!

Your career center has a unique opportunity to become the center of the campus experience, but it won't happen, unless you start to put it "in the clouds."

"Know thyself"

-Ancient Greek Aphorism

IMMERSE STUDENTS IN PERSONAL REFLECTION, CAREER EVALUATION AND SELF-STUDY

How many of your students are taking advantage of your career and personality assessments?

One of the first immersive experiences we suggest you provide incoming freshman is to take a series of personality, behavior, interest and skills tests so they can gain a better understanding of not only their personalities but how to communicate and work with others who have different personalities.

One of the challenges you face is getting students to take assessments. Consider adopting an incentive programs, extracurricular credit, or even contests offered to increase participation. You could also utilize social media, campus ambassadors, testimonials, alumni participation and campus reminders to encourage participation.

We suggest you carefully develop a strategy that will deliver career related information to students each year.

For example:

- The freshman year is a good time to help students understand their own interests, skills, passions, behaviors and personalities so they can begin to explore the types of industries, jobs, and responsibilities in which they will succeed. Besides offering assessments, students should be offered self-study courses on career exploration and learning on how to look for jobs.

- The sophomore years is a good time to connect students with alumni and give them access to courses about networking and building professional relationships using LinkedIn and even Facebook.

- During their junior years, students should be focusing on building their resumes around the skills, accomplishments, leadership positions, and projects they've that have been part of their educations.

- Of course, students' senior years should be spent learning how to look for jobs, the things different industries look for, and how to interview and follow up on interviews.

Additionally the college needs to help students understand how what they are learning can be applied in a business environment and how to communicate those skills in job interviews. Faculty of philosophy, political science and art majors, as examples, must understand that the vast majority of their students will NOT get a job in their fields, but will need to know how to apply the knowledge they do receive across multiple industries and job functions. It's not something that will fundamentally change the curriculum of the faculty, but it will enable the students to use their knowledge bases to build their careers and job search strategies as they move through their college educations.

These are only suggestions to get you thinking about what would be best for your graduates and are not meant to be offered as the only strategies you should implement.

Get your team together and identify strategies that fit your college culture, faculty interests, students' needs and the overall mission of your college.

The ancient Greek aphorism, "Know thyself," is as important today as it was 3,000 years ago. The better your students understand who they are and where their skills will best fit, the happier and more successful they will be.

Your career center has to provide relevant, compelling and cloud-driven career advice if you want students to take personal ownership of their careers.

"All men are caught in an inescapable network of mutuality."

-Martin Luther King Jr.

CONNECT STUDENTS WITH A MINIMUM OF 40 ALUMNI BY GRADUATION DAY

There are thousands of successful alumni who may be willing to dedicate time to mentoring current students and recent grads.

In the past, it was nearly impossible to connect willing alumni and students. The typical alumni association that even bothered with an alumni mentor program kept a 3-ring binder and found it nearly impossible to manage the process.

LinkedIn will reach 275 million users by the end of 2014 and Facebook has already passed the 1 billion users mark.

Both of these databases offer a unique opportunity to bring alumni and students together. Imagine a staff member sitting at a computer all day long and their sole job is to introduce alumni to each other on these and other online communities.

Alumni associations may try to get the career center involved in their alumni online community but we highly suggest you resist that. Alumni online communities are literal ghost towns and frankly are a waste of college resources.

Regardless of what system you end up using to connect and engage alumni and students, you have to be proactive and introduce people to each other!

The Stanford Shyness Clinic suggests 60 percent of us are shy. That shyness prevents us from asking questions in classes, introducing ourselves at social events, and even extends into our virtual lives. Your students and alumni will LOVE being introduced to others who have similar interests or are on similar career paths.

One introduction can literally change a life!

We suggest during their freshman years, students be required to build their LinkedIn profiles so your team can begin to introduce them to alumni. To be successful, both participating alumni and students should sign commitments and have a clear understanding of what is expected of them. Your alumni can either attend a live webinar or watch a video recording which outlines what is expected of them as a mentor. Your students can either pick up this information from one of the courses you offer or watch on-demand videos that provide details on how to be mentored!

You can increase Internships!

A side benefit of increasing contact with alumni is that you put in motion more conversations and discussions that could result in internships between the students and their mentors. Internships are rapidly becoming an important bullet on resumes. Students with Internships are getting hired, while students without internships are having to overcome the deficit by differentiating themselves in other ways.

A survey by InternBridge of 18,000 college students found that 60 percent indicated that their colleges are requiring internships. If this trend continues, you need to find ways to make it easier for your students to get internships.

Shawn Brown, Associate Director of Northeast Ohio Council on Higher Education, works closely with businesses to remind them of the benefits of providing internships and even offers programs to teach businesses how to make internships a successful experience for both. He has over 10,000 students willing to participate in internships.

According to Shawn:

> "Alumni associations are the bridge the career center needs to cross to get access to open-armed alumni who would be more than willing to mentor students. Successful colleges in the future will need to

proactively "invent" opportunities to bring alumni and students together online."

Teach students how to interact and engage with alumni!

We encourage you to develop programs where students write biographies of their mentors as part of a class project or track their mentors' companies in Google Alerts so they can ask questions about their mentors' professions and companies.

##

Martin Luther King reminded us that we are intricately dependent on each other. The greatest strength colleges have is in their alumni networks. Anything you can do to encourage the connection of your students with alumni will pay off 10 fold.

Your alumni are the key to your students' internships and your graduates' first jobs. Focus on building these relationships.

"The highest reward for a person's toil is not what they get from it, but what they become by it"

-John Ruskin

PROVIDE A CORE CAREER CURRICULUM

We discussed at length how graduating seniors are clueless about what it takes to find a job.

Tony Beshara, author of *The Job Search Solution* and an employment specialist who has personally placed 8,000 people in jobs over 3 decades spoke at our GRAD Career Webinar Series and told students:

- It takes 100 phone calls to reach 10 hiring managers of which 2 will have jobs available

- It will take them on average 16 interviews to get jobs! (see page 26)

If students don't have access to curriculum and "frank" talk that provides them the facts of what it takes to get a job, their chances of getting a job diminish. In fact they end up wasting a great deal of time and in many cases working harder, not smarter.

Don Peck in his book, *The Next Economy* suggests, "Holding out for the perfect job is likely to turn out poorly for most people. "In 2008, fewer people moved, as a percentage for the population, than any year on record." Peck speculates that Millennials are staying close to home because of the financial and emotional support available from family and friends. Parents may be better advised to encourage their kids to look for jobs outside the family nest.

Online education is really nothing new
– but it is for career education.

Nearly every college is developing online courses that complement the existing courses offered on campus or they are building new online degree programs using emerging e-learning platforms.

The Sloan report we mentioned in a preceding chapter collected data from more than 2,500 colleges and universities.

One of the key summaries was:

> Bad economic times, which traditionally drive more people back to school, are having a particularly strong impact on demand for online courses. Seventy-three percent of institutions report increased demand for existing online courses, compared with 54 percent for face-to-face. Sixty-six percent report increased demand for new online courses... and students are clamoring for distance education at colleges that don't offer it; 45 percent of institutions in that category report growing demand for new online courses and programs.

Despite this increase in demand for online courses, few institutions are developing online courses in career exploration, job searches, networking, interviewing, building one's personal brand or using social media in the job search.

In order to increase the amount of time and attention students spend on their career preparation while keeping staffing affordable, we think it will be critical for your college to offer career courses online.

By offering career courses online:

- You will be able to track use and frequency

- You can compare those results with speed of employment and pay rate.

- You can reach more students anytime, anyplace and through any device.

- You can provide "master teachers" at ridiculously low costs per student.

Plus, if you were adopting the TalentMarks e-Learning platform, you'd be able to offer the top career authors and experts as your career faculty.

In his quote at the beginning of this chapter, John Ruskin reminds us that the richness of one's life is not measured by what he or she had, but what he or she had become. Your faculty, administrators, coaches, club directors and everyone on campus has the potential to help your students interpret what they are learning in religion or engineering or any other field and translate it into the skills, knowledge and behaviors to help them live their dreams.

Why does the career center have to be the last department on campus with an e-learning strategy?

"It takes a village to educate a child."

-Hillary Clinton

INTEGRATE CAREER LEARNING OPPORTUNITIES WITH CLASSES

Hillary Clinton reminded us that it "takes a village to educate a child."

We share that vision when it comes to preparing students for their careers. One lone career professional doesn't have a chance in making a significant difference in hundreds of graduates' lives, but a collective team of faculty, administrators, athletic coaches and career professionals, working together *can*.

An important element of the career centered college culture will be to gain the cooperation and interest of faculty and staff members to build in assignments that will help reinforce the need for students to understand how the information they are learning can be used in building their career strategies.

Let's take a look at a few examples:

1. The English class, journalism, or PR class could require the students to write a bio about one of their alumni mentors. The instructor could identify what would be required, the content, length, questions to be asked etc. This will enable the student to gain a better understanding of the mentor's job function, daily activities, and responsibilities. These bios could be shared on the admissions website as well as the alumni website as a way to recognize and reward alumni for their career contributions and volunteerism.

2. The psychology professor could ask students to do a report that identifies what each learned about personality types from their Platinum Rule Behavior Tests. The professor could ask them to write the report in relation to the type of personalities future employers might have and to discuss how the student would adapt to such a personality.

3. Students in an English class might be required to participate in a class blog that focuses on a specific industry. Students would be required to set Google Alerts to deliver breaking news, capture press releases and updates from other sources, and then write blog articles about the information to exercise thought leadership skills.

4. Your speech faculty could also incorporate interviewing techniques as an assignment. Students would be required to watch online e-Learning courses on interviewing and then use that knowledge to interview one another in class.

5. Your alumni association or fraternal organizations could offer young alumni meetings where they give students practice at implementing some of the networking techniques they learn via the on-demand e-Learning courses.

6. Marketing and business majors could be asked to create social media strategies for alumni businesses. Students have intuitive knowledge about how to use social media that small business owners lack. Students would not only gain first hand experience in using tools they love, but they'll end up helping alumni who are confused and not sure how to implement a social media strategies themselves. The benefits? Alumni gain knowledge and access to a new marketing channel that rings their cash register while you build a bridge connecting the students to possible long-term relationships with these contacts that may well provide internships and jobs in the future.

7. Athletic coaches could use their pulpits to require students to build an understanding of leadership into their career strategies, as well as identify how critical it is for a team of people to work beyond their differences and focus on the objectives of the team.

Unfortunately this strategy will take time. First, you have to get upper management to support the strategy and put some teeth behind it. Next, you need to get faculty to come together and brainstorm guidelines, methodologies and accepted ways to introduce how to translate what they are teaching into nuggets of skills, knowledge and techniques to support the goals of your graduates' future employers.

Like any new initiatives, you'll run into dead ends and have to figure out how to get where you want to go. Remember, we are trying to change the culture on campus so that *everyone* is doing your job, not just little ole' you!

##

Hillary Clinton reminds us that it takes everyone in the village to educate and prepare youth to accept their positions within the community. You have a unique opportunity to bring together others on campus to share the responsibility of preparing your graduates.

Take a moment to think about different ways you can integrate career curriculum.

"If you don't have a strategy, you're part of someone else's strategy."

-Alvin Toffler

REQUIRE STUDENTS TO WRITE CAREER AND JOB SEARCH PLANS

Research conducted by TalentMarks indicates that 95 percent of college grads don't have clear (if any) career/job search strategies. That might have worked for the classes of 2007 and prior, when the labor market was strong, but frankly today's graduates cannot "wing it."

Besides graduating into a very uncertain and competitive job market, according to the Department of Labor, students today will have 11-14 jobs by the time they are 38 years old. When studies indicate looking for a job is one of the most stressful activities in human history, it only makes sense that we give students the skills to "work smarter, not harder," through their job transitions.

Many of the professors and staff on our campuses today, started their first job searches by picking up relevant newspapers and newsletters and sitting down at the kitchen table to circle 140-character ads and make phone calls.

Today's graduates have a myriad of emerging strategies. It's important to remember that strategies that work in some industries will not in others. In order to successfully transition from their job searches to work, graduates will need to develop the discipline of developing relationships with alumni, classmates, friends and colleagues.

According to Diane Darling, author of the books, *the Networking Survival Guide* and *Networking for Career Success*:

"Careers are stifled and in many cases ruined because people have not been taught to network. Introverts miss out on incredible lifelong business relationships because they were too shy to introduce themselves or failed to follow up on an introduction, and extroverts blow opportunities because they 'asked first' and didn't give value to emerging relationships. College and universities will produce more successful graduates if they educate them in the proven steps to professionally network."

The process we've been discussing would require students to slowly --over their four year experiences-- build their career strategies and job search plans. Studies indicate that when you plan something in writing, it is more likely to be accomplished.

Your students should have completed by their senior years personal documents that identifies:

•   Their personality types and what careers would provide the best fit

•   Their behavior styles so they can know what adjustments they need to make in their communication with people who have different styles

•   A pros and cons list outlining different job functions and careers that are real possibilities

•   Networking strategies

•   Job search strategies

•   Career strategies that will outline what they want to achieve in the next 5 years (including those years after graduation).

While your organization can create forms to accomplish this, an online version of the program would be ideal as it can:

•   Remind students to complete items as deadlines approach

•   Quickly show coaches and advisors students' posts, histories, discussions, and student progress

•   Provide a lifetime resource for students/alumni that is automatically updated

These could even be used to offer students suggestions about what information or skills they will need to achieve their goals and strategies.

To encourage students to build career strategies, consider offering a guarantee like Thomas College offers. Here's how they explain it to their students:

The Guaranteed Job Placement program was launched at Thomas in 1999 and is the only one of its kind in New England. It the most extensive guarantee offered by any college or university in the United States. If you don't secure employment within six months after graduation, you can come back to Thomas to for **up to two more years, tuition-free,** or we'll pay the monthly payment for your **federally subsidized student loans** that you incurred while attending Thomas College for up to one year or until you land that first job.

Even better, if you are employed within six months following graduation, but the position is not within your field of study (you decide that - for whatever reason), you can still choose to come back to Thomas and take an unlimited number of **tuition-free** undergraduate courses for up to two years or you can choose to take up to half of the graduate courses required to complete any one of the Master's degree programs at Thomas - again, **tuition-free!**

That's a pretty incredible guarantee!

Because the career center is no more than a campus club and participation is optional, you will need to look at doing innovative things to encourage students to focus on their career explorations and job search strategies.

You don't have to go the distance to offer a guarantee, but you could provide certificates grads could share with employers that show they have completed a rigorous program to prepare them for the campus-to-corporate transition, or even offer them more advanced career center services that might include:

- Introductions to alumni

- More one-on-one coaching

A few well thought-out incentives will definitely get students' attention and increase participation.

Alvin Toffler reminds us that if you do not have a strategy, you are part of someone else's strategy. Without strategies, your students will wander, waist time and not live up to their potentials. Your quest to create a career centered college campus, will never happen unless you create a strategy.

Assuming your grads have 14 job hunts each ahead of them during the 15 years after college, you could help reduce their economic pain and personal stress if you made sure they KNEW how to search for a job before they graduated

"A coach is someone who tells you what you don't want to hear, who has you see what you don't want to see, so you can be who you have always known you could be."

-Tom Landry

BUILD A CAREER SUPPORT TEAM FOR STUDENTS AND GRADS

It's hard to provide one-on-one counseling to all the students to whom you are assigned.

According to the National Association of Colleges and Employers:

- The average ratio of students to full-time professional staff was calculated to be 2,890 students per FTE staff member.

- The average ratio of students per career counselor is 9,377 students per counselor.

- The average number of counseling appointments per career counselor is 1,863.

It's clear under the present budgeting process the career center does not receive enough resources to provide meaningful and dedicated career advising to students in any of their four years of college.

In a previous white paper *10 Ways to Get More Resources for Your career center*, we went through a long analysis that suggested that a college that adhered to this staffing ratio, would result in – at best – a grad receiving 1.6 hours of career coaching or advising.

That's barely enough to help a student develop his or her resume.

Research conducted by Stanford University Associate Professor Eric Bettinger that reviewed the academic records of more than 13,500 students from 8 college campuses including the 2003-4 and 2007-8 academic years, suggests that career coaching can make a sizeable impact on retention, graduation rates and students' success. His findings showed a:

- 10% increase in retention after six months which increased to 15% after 18 months

- 13% increase in graduation rates with career coaching

The one-on-one coaching required to reach these numbers is not cheap, but it is more effective than increasing financial aid to students! According to Bettinger's study:

> "A $1,000 increase in financial aid typically increases persistence by three percentage points, while a two-semester investment in one-on-one coaching costs about the same and increases persistence by five percentage points."

Students in this study received in-person, one-on-one coaching to achieve these results.

However, there are alternative ways to deliver personal coaching and surround students with a group of caring supporters who will help them keep their eyes on the proverbial ball.

In the 2nd initiative we discussed, we suggested that students get introduced and connected to a minimum of 40 alumni with similar majors and are who are working in careers where those students' interests lie.

We would suggest that a requirement of an alum mentor is to invest 2-3 hours a year with the student he or she is assigned. This can be done in webcam discussions, phone calls, emails or personal visits.

We also think a more formal coaching program can be setup and delivered cost effectively using technology and professionally certified coaches and or retired alumni who go through a certification process. For this to be successful, you will need to develop an overall strategy outlining what coaches will cover each year and what they should discuss so that you can keep a uniform and consistent program.

Both faculty and staff could and should be part of the overall coaching initiative. In many ways, faculty are already serving this role successfully.

The automated data capture system we suggested in the previous point could also serve for coaches to keep notes, compare strategies and provide a group of people to serve as student coaches more quickly or even on-demand.

Finally we think parents have a role in helping students stay focused on developing their career plans. They should receive updates and be provided access (with their students' permission) to their students' career plans and progress. In many cases, they are footing the bill and should be notified if their students are not taking part in the career development part of their educations.

Tom Landry's quote reminds us of the importance of coaches in our lives. Your athletic coaches push, drive and collectively work on your athletes to help them accomplish more then they could have ever done on their own. Find a way to connect students with alumni and provide more coaching to your students.

"One if the hardest things in life is to learn are which bridges to cross and which bridges to burn."

-Oprah Winfrey

THE EMPLOYERS OF YOUR ALUMNI ARE YOUR NEW GOLD MINE!

Colleges and universities have alumni working in organizations around the world. If you have 20,000 alumni, there may be anywhere from 8,000-10,000 organizations for which they work.

You have an incredible opportunity to harness your alumni's influence and position within these organizations to increase internships and the hiring of your graduates. We've seen successful models where alumni associations have developed company/alumni "affinity groups."

These organizations had four goals when they started company/alumni affinity groups.

They wanted to:

1. Raise the awareness and prestige of the college within the company.

2. Increase the number of student interns and grads hired.

3. Enroll more employees in the company in their advanced degree programs.

4. Reach parents of students who would soon be looking at colleges.

To launch the program, databases were sorted to find alumni who were working in the same company and instituted a direct mail, email, and phone call campaign to each. In some cases, depending on the number of alumni at the company, a personal visit was also in order.

The ramifications of pursuing this strategy were enormous.

By emulating it, you will first build pride and enthusiasm for alumni within a specific company, you will then get them acting as reminders of the quality interns and grads you have, and finally you will help admissions by delivering their message to prospective students, their parents and others looking for advanced degrees!

Brilliant!

Once you have a program like this in place, you can even take it one step further by offering to subsidize the hourly pay of interns.

Imagine if you could tell your alumni that if their firm hired an intern, the college will subsidize 20-50% of their pay. You'd have employers lining up to take your graduates. A program like this would help supercharge your annual giving program as it gives your phone callers a marketing message and a powerful edge that resonates with alumni. Take some time to decide how to build bridges to the companies with which your alumni are working and concentrate more time and energy on them.

Oprah Winfrey's quote reminds us to question if the things we are investing time in today are providing the right kinds of return that and are required to help our students get internships, our grads get jobs, and our alumni lead successful careers. You might need to give up some old relationships to concentrate on new, more promising relationships with the firms that hire your graduates.

Your alumni association has the ability to infiltrate thousands of businesses and to use them as recruiting, fundraising and employment partners.

"The greatest gift you can give a person is a job!"

-Bernie Schneier

PUT YOUR CAREER CENTER UNDER A DIFFERENT DEPARTMENT

The vast majority of colleges and universities have placed the career center under student services on their organization chart.

This seems to have made sense over the years. After all, the career center works directly with students and by having it report to student services, and it gives the career center a better shot at getting access to students via various channels like events, residence halls, etc. Another group of colleges has put the career center under the academic wing. Still a very small minority are beginning to put the career center under the development department.

That idea is not new.

Richard Bolles, author of *What Color is Your Parachute?* suggested over 35 years ago that, "Working alumni are giving alumni!" Alumni with not only jobs-- but successful careers -- will have the resources to give of their time, treasures and their talents!

By placing the career center under the development office, you open up a number of interesting new opportunities.

1. It will be easier to get the alumni office and career center working more closely with one another to build mentorships and internships.

2. You can reach out to alumni to support initiatives and extracurricular career activities that may not have been funded by the general college budget.

3. You could raise money from alumni to subsidize student internships so companies could hire them for a lower hourly wage – or no wage at all.

Juniata College, a small liberal arts college, was among the first colleges in the country to offer a 4-year college graduation guarantee. They understood that in order to be competitive and offer a fair value to their students and the parents of those students, they needed to do everything in their power to make sure students were able to finish college in 4 years. If they didn't, students could continue for free until they graduated.

Juniata College is now taking steps to improve their graduates' chances of getting jobs.

Recently they moved their career center to report to the development office and the direct supervision of the Executive Director of Constituent Relations, Linda Carpenter. According to Linda,

> "Even though 60 percent of our graduates have a job by graduation day, we believe we can do better. We believe one of our greatest assets to help grads get jobs is our alumni network. Our move to put our career center under the development office will increase the points of contact between students and alumni. It keeps us thinking about helping alumni build successful careers before we think about asking them to contribute."

You have to decide what will work best for your department.

This kind of move can only occur if the development office passionately believes they can open channels and build connections with alumni, the businesses with whom alumni work, and the students on campus. From our perspective, this can't hurt!

Pay for internships

The third point we mentioned above involved offering to subsidize your students' intern pay to encourage more companies to hire them.

It's a relatively new concept, but a few colleges have developed funds that pay all or a part of an interns' wages.

The College of Holy Cross in Massachusetts introduced this concept a number of years ago. Its Leadership Council of New York decided to create a "rainy day" fund for the college's summer internship program. As the economic and employment crash unfolded in 2008 and 2009, and businesses that traditionally hired their interns had to pass, the council was able to reach into its fund and give the alumni director the discretion to offer to pay for the students' wages to companies who could not afford to do so that year. According to Amy Murphy, Director of Summer Internships,

> "It was an unbelievable position for me to be able to tell employers that, in this economy, we would supplement them for a year," she explains. "We were able to help them financially and provide valuable opportunities for our students. We demonstrated to these employers that, clearly, we are committed to our relationships with them."

It's a fantastic idea really, and you could build into it a carrot and stick technique to make sure students are working on their career plans. Consider making this type of program only available to students who have completed specific steps in their career and job search plans. In the last section, we provided an outline of things students should be doing each year. If you used it as a template for your strategy, then students who completed the required steps by the end of their sophomore years would qualify for summer internship programs where an approved company could hire them and --depending on how you set it up-- pay only half their hourly wage if anything.

Changing the entity to which the career center reports might be a bigger hurdle than you want to take on initially. We are not suggesting that you have to implement all of the 10 steps we are recommending at one time. If you like this idea, you can begin to introduce it over time and continue to offer examples and reasons why it should happen.

##

I think of Bernie Schneier's quote frequently. A job enables a person to start a family and care for them, to explore their hobbies and interests and to help others, including your college. Your college would be ahead of the rest if the sole focus, the sole purpose, and number one goal of your institution is to help all grads and alumni who want jobs get jobs. You have to take an innovative approach to change your culture and realign the resources to give your students a shot at internships, mentoring relationships, and the resources and knowledge they need to succeed.

"If you're ridin' ahead of the herd, take a look back every now and then to make sure it's still there"

- Will Rogers

CHAPTER SUMMARY

If you've made it to the summary, you must realize your college could be doing more to help grads and alumni build successful careers.

Your next steps are simple!

Pull a team together to start discussing how you can put the career center at the center of the college and university's activities.

To change your culture, and the opinions that have traditionally been held for decades is going take time, effort and commitment. It won't be easy, but somebody has to pick up the challenge. Your passion and compassion for the plights of students and grads will help you overcome the nay-sayers, roadblocks and setbacks.

Michael Jordan once said:

> "I've missed more than 9,000 shots in my career. I've lost almost 300 games. 26 times, I've been trusted to take the game's winning shot and missed. I've failed over and over and over again in my life... and that is why I succeed."

Michael did this in a very public forum! Millions of people watched each of the moments he describes and everyone that watched gasped, moaned and screamed at him when he missed the 26 game winning shots. Don't be afraid to make mistakes! After all, if your college is like most colleges, it is already failing a huge number of graduates. Anything you are doing is a step in the right direction.

Your college is already spending millions on retention, sports, entertainment, and guest speakers. You deserve to have the resources to implement the strategies that will have a profound effect on graduates' lives for decades to come.

To move this process in time to be of help to your current and future grads, you need to move quickly and publicly.

You'll need to take a lot of shots to get this process started, but once you do, I'm convinced you will start a snowball reaction that WILL have the greatest impact on the success of not only your graduates and alumni, but the reputation and success of your college!

Act on your passion and keep taking shots!

It's the right thing to do.

"Make your mistakes, next year and forever."

— Neil Gaiman

5 | 10 IDEAS TO SHAPE YOUR DEPARTMENT'S FUTURE

This is the year to STOP budget cuts in your department!

I love the 1976 movie *Network* featuring Fay Dunaway, William Holden and Peter Finch. Peter received a posthumous Oscar for Best Performance for an Actor in a Leading Role for his portrayal as a mad profit of the airways who challenged his viewers around the nation to get mad about the issues they were facing.

Peter acted as a catalyst for people to stand up for themselves and do something about environmental issues, the constant fear of unemployment, and punks running wild in the streets.

In his role as Howard Beale, Peter is noted for the line,

> "I want you to get up right now and go to the window, open it and stick your head out and yell 'I'm as mad as hell and I'm not going to take it anymore.'"

Take a moment right now and go to YouTube and search for – "Peter Finch mad as hell." I guarantee it will make you want to go to your window and yell,

"I'm mad as hell and I'm:

- not going to take a budget cut this year!"

- not going to give up another staff position."

- going to find a way to get more students take ownership of their careers!"

- going to get others on campus to support a career initiative!"

Whatever you end up yelling, it will be a cathartic moment and I know you will feel better. But for now, I want you to take a look as some initiatives and ideas that will help you build a vision that your management team can buy into. I want you to pick and choose one or two ideas that you can build a strategy around, something that is exciting, that matches the vision and mission, as well as the current objectives of your administration, and one that you are passionate about.

Then put together a quick report and share it with management!

Oh, and stay mad! It's a great motivator.

Here are my favorite new initiatives.

1. Start a First Year GRAD Experience for Your Graduates!
2. Career centers' Future? Charge Fees for Levels of Service
3. Your President Is Going TO LOVE "Shared Services" for Career Services
4. Career services "in the cloud" accessible by mobile devices
5. Get Parents to Work For Your Career Center
6. 3 Reasons to Start a Campus Career Club
7. Proven Way to Help More Grads Prepare for Job Search
8. Performance Based Funding - What Your Career Center Needs to Know!
9. Find Out What Your Customers Think of Your Career Center
10. Hel Alumni Build Successful Careers

GRADS NEED HELP IN THE TRANSITION FROM CAMPUS TO CORPORATE LIFE

First Year Grad Experience Gives Grads Soft Skills

Your college has a unique opportunity to build a stronger relationship with recent grads by adopting a First Year GRAD Experience. The FYGE would offer graduates access to career advice, information and curriculum anytime through any device as they transition from college to corporate life. Few grads are prepared for this transition.

Few grads have the skills to search for jobs, handle finances and manage the stresses of supporting themselves. All grads will struggle with some aspect of the campus to corporate transition.

There is a precedent for this idea.

Your college probably has a First Year Experience (FYE) program.
The National Resource Center for The First-Year Experience and Students in Transition was founded 32 years ago at the University of South Carolina by John Gardner to advance and support efforts to improve student learning and transitions into, and through, higher education. I got involved in the program nearly 20 years ago when I was promoting the use of photo business cards as a way for students to meet, remember each other's names, and network with more students. The goal was to use business cards as a way to help students develop more friends so they would be less likely to drop out in the critical first 6 weeks.

The FYE program has been recognized for increasing retention and helping students manage the transition faster, with fewer issues. As a result, the effort is supported by staff and budgets, and it is embedded into the curriculum, organization, and cultures of campuses.

Your grads are facing significant campus to career transition issues! A recent survey by the Career Advisory Board of over 600 career directors found that:

• 48.1% thought students did not have the knowledge they needed to find jobs.

• 55.7% felt students resumes were not professional enough to use for their job searches.

I keep going back to this industry study because it is screaming that something is broken and needs to be fixed. Career directors correctly suggest in the report that one way to fix the problem is requiring students to take career courses while in college. The problem all cite, however, is that it is extremely difficult to get the administration and faculty behind the idea. The chances of adding career courses to the current curriculum in the next 5 years is slim to none.

An alternative solution is for your alumni association to adopt a First Year GRAD Experience program.

The alumni association and the career center could collaborate on a program that will provide a ramped up, post-graduation career program that will give idle grads an opportunity to hone their interviewing skills and knowledge about how to find jobs.

I would encourage your alumni association to take the lead on this program for two reasons:

1. It will give them the opportunity to build a relationship with alumni that is NOT associated with fundraising.

2. It will build a culture within your alumni association of giving back, mentoring and helping students get jobs.

With limited resources and staffing, this strategy helps you keep the career center focused on students and gives the alumni association the responsibility to reach out and engage recent grads with this program. In the end, the development office benefits.

Richard Bolles, author of the book, What's The Color of Your Parachute? once said, *"A working alum is a giving alum!"*

So how do you get started?

Simple!

1. Find out if you have a FYE program on your campus.

2. If you do, get an idea about the size of their staff and budget

I'd like you to start a discussion on your campus to question why the campus is not supporting grads in their transition from college to corporate life. They have trusted your college and rewarded it with $80,000 or more! Your college can't just sit on its hands and consider it "a job well done." Your college is not done until every graduate has a job!

Your graduates' needs are significant and the issues they face are great! Remind those you report to that a FYE program was introduced 32 years ago to solve a problem for the college and it's time the college solves a number of problems grads are facing!

Be among the first movers in this area by starting discussions today. Talk to students and get the young alumni group to pick this up as a project. Quite frequently, if an idea shows strong support by students, and it makes sense, more people will get behind it!

It's the right thing to do!

But, you need to act fast there are careers and lives at stake!

CAREER CENTERS' FUTURE? CHARGE FEES FOR LEVELS OF SERVICE

Offer existing services as standard and then charge for "deluxe" services

Your President will find this concept intriguing.

I realize this could be a controversial topic in your department, but in light of the pressures your college is facing, it's something your college will eventually have to implement. Here's my prediction. Your college will, at some time in the foreseeable future, charge students to provide them with the level of service and outcome they and their parents expect from their college investment.

Think about it for a moment.

Almost anything a student does on-campus comes at an additional cost. As a parent, I feel it every time I pay tuition, room and board, books, student fees, club fees, transportation fees, and parking. I feel it when I buy athletic/entertainment or guest speaker tickets, pay for health services, or incur any of the sundry fees now included in the college experience. Everything costs! So why not charge me to provide my kids' career services? Consider continuing to offer the current services that you offer for free, but charge for more advanced services.

We discussed earlier that your career center could be facing legislation that will require you to prove your grads are "gainfully employed" in jobs that are relevant to their degrees, as well as pay enough for them to cover living expenses and at the same time pay down their student loans. We also discussed the expectations of your parents and students, which are on the rise.

In order for you to get ahead of this issue and hire more counselors and staff and provide more resources, you will need a bigger budget. If you are like most career centers you are facing yearly budget freezes or-- more likely--budget cuts.

In order to help offset the costs of hiring additional staff, and buying curriculum, videos and other tools necessary to help students explore career options and build successful career strategies, consider adopting a tiered services program. You could come up with a good, better, and best option that parents and students could choose from. The fee might be included as a line item charge on the tuition bill, or it might be a separate charge, just like buying books.

Charging students for career services is already being done in California.

The Chancellor of the California State University system has authorized a number of CSU colleges to charge a "Student Success" fee. At California State University Polytechnics (CalPoly), students are now paying $410 per year for university services related to their career success. Each CSU college is given the flexibility to determine where these funds are used. Some of the funding goes to academic advising and related "retention" programs.

Based on this experience, it might make sense to give students and parents the options of deciding where they want to spend their money.

Charging a fee, whether it's optional or required, does two things. First, with additional resources, the career center is able to ramp up services and curriculum and become more inventive about how to increase students' use of the services. It will give the career center the ability to add staff to engage alumni, place students in companies, track employment results, reach out to more companies, and provide more one-on-one coaching.

The second advantage is an increased use of your services. If parents are paying for advanced career services, it's likely they will be more engaged in making sure their children are utilizing them.

You've heard the old adage, "You get what you pay for!"

Will parents and students pay for "deluxe" career services? The simple answer is yes. The same parents spend as little as a couple of hundred, and others as much as $10,000, to provide their son or daughter SAT and ACT coaching and training. I can guarantee these same parents and others will understand the value of giving their student the skills and knowledge they need to lead successful careers.

What can we expect if you don't charge fees?

It's no secret to anyone who is working in the career center that the department has never had enough funding and resources to serve all students. The average career center counselor is responsible to coach and advise 1,645 students, which makes it literally impossible to even offer 1 hour of career advising to each student in a year. The average career center has an operating budget of only $63,086 per year. (The median operating budget is considerably smaller at only $31,000 per year)

It's clear in today's tight economic times that the career center is going to face ongoing budget cuts. Charging fees is the only way the career center is going to be able to maintain service levels!

Is this the right direction for your college?

1. Do some research and look at what your colleagues are doing at their colleges. You need to create a benchmark with which to compare yourself.

2. Create a short memo for your boss and get his/her feedback on what you need to do --give management enough details they can help make a decision.

3. Create an outline of what your basic, free service will be and what advantages a better and best product will offer.

Fee based services offer your career center enormous opportunities to change the paradigm and offer transformative innovation with the administration's blessings! It will give you a change to offer a variety of services to students and give them the flexibility to opt-in to the program that best fits their needs.

YOUR PRESIDENT IS GOING TO LOVE "SHARED SERVICES" FOR CAREER SERVICES

Save money, yet increase services 24/7 to more students & increase staff

Over the past decade college presidents have been under pressure to cut costs and find ways to generate revenue.

One way colleges have been cutting costs is by finding ways to outsource tasks, or share services, that are unrelated to the core competencies of those colleges. Today over 1,500 colleges and universities have partnered with either Barnes or Noble, or Follett, to manage their bookstores, and another 500 colleges have outsourced their computer help desks to companies. Colleges are also exploring ways they can share noncompetitive administrative costs including payroll and programming.

In an article in Educause, Luis M. Proenza, President of The University of Akron and Roy A. Church, President of Lorain County Community College writes:

"In these challenging economic times, colleges and universities must work together to attain academic and operational successes. The shared-services approach can help higher education institutions cut costs and better serve their students, faculty, staff, and communities. It is a model that can allow institutions to stay focused on the core missions of teaching, learning, and research. Partnerships and collaboration are the keys to the future of higher education in Ohio and in the world."

A new area colleges and universities are exploring is sharing services in their career centers.

Investments in the career center have been traditionally small per student in relation to recruitment and other student services investments. For example, the average private college will spend over $3,000 to recruit each freshman student. With a larger marketing budget and bigger class size, the average state college will spend over $1,000 to recruit each freshman. Yet surveys by the National Association of Colleges and Employers show that in both state and private colleges, the average career center has less than $100 to spend to prepare seniors for their first professional job searches. If you spread their resources to include freshman, sophomores and juniors (who should be working on their career strategy) that number would be less than $25 per student.

We are living in a time where pressure from legislatures, parents, students and the media will require management to increase funding and resources to the career center. The legislature is increasingly holding college management's feet to the fire to find ways to increase the number of students that:

• Graduate.

• Graduate on time.

• Graduate with a job.

Surveys of parents and students are evaluating majors and colleges on their abilities to ensure their grads have a job by graduation day. In this new environment, in order to be competitive in recruiting and to match the demands of a new consumer and political environment, career centers will need to hire more career advisors, provide online career courses and content, and develop a four-year curriculum that students can follow which will ensure they have completed the steps necessary to explore career opportunities, acquire job search skills, create written career plans and build professional networks. This could easily reach $200,000 for a small college and could amount to over $750,000 for larger colleges and universities.

While private colleges have to balance their budgets and get approval for expenditures from their boards, and for-profit colleges ultimately get approval from their shareholders, the future of state colleges will be determined by the government entities providing them ever diminishing funding.

The Ohio legislature established an advisory committee that is coordinated by the Board of Regents Chancellor, Jim Petro. The Efficiency Advisory Committee is comprised of 40 people representing each state institution of higher education. It meets quarterly to discuss ways to generate optimal efficiency plans for campuses, while at the same time identifying shared service opportunities and best practices. The newly formed committee (Its first meeting was in September 2012,) is challenged to look at ways to not only reduce the cost of education for students and their families by reducing overhead, but to also improve the quality of service.

The shared-services concept is being accepted around the globe. HE-Shared Services Ltd (HE-SS) was formed in 2008 to help the 166 colleges and universities in the United Kingdom find ways in which they could identify significant efficiencies and help large IT vendors understand more about how the Higher Education sector is structured and works.

Forward thinking colleges are also exploring this opportunity on their own campuses. Jim Sage, CIO of The University of Akron, is frequently called on by his president to find ways to cut costs. Jim has pioneered a number of shared-services projects. According to Jim,

> "Colleges and universities like ours are evaluating what our core competencies are and beginning to realize that with limited resources, increased competition, and increased expectations of our constituents and customers, we need to adopt strategies that increase customer satisfaction while at the same time reducing costs."

A shared-services approach will not change the way career centers operate. Centers would still advise and coach students, and organize and manage career fairs campus visits, and resume coaching. However, a shared-services approach could provide the career center with new technology, career curriculum, website management, marketing services to increase student participation, and career webinars, along with more analytics of effectiveness and even "overflow" career coaching during busy periods. In addition, it could offer more anytime-anywhere services including providing more services to graduates who are looking for jobs.

A centralized shared-service program can be branded so that resources, courses and materials will have the college logo and brand. It can be designed to provide marketing expertise that few college career professionals have time to acquire, to increase the buzz, excitement and student commitment to building career strategies.

By not having to duplicate services and hire more staff, the career center can remain nimble, reach more students, and at the same time provide more services. On top of that a shared-services approach is predicted to cut expected cost increases mentioned above by as much as seventy percent.

Should you be moving in this direction?

While I'd say yes, here are a couple of things you can do to see if this strategy is the right one for your college:

1. Identify the type of services, tools and coaching you think will be necessary to stay competitive (if not a leader), and help more grads get jobs by graduation day.

2. Determine which strategies could be implemented faster, and at a lower annual cost, by adopting a shared services model.

3. Develop a business and implementation plan and present it to your management.

Now that you have a plan, you will be able to make a greater impact on a greater number of students sooner than later!

CAREER SERVICES "IN THE CLOUD" ACCESSIBLE BY MOBILE DEVICES

*Your career center is no longer a destination
– meet students where they are*

The career center has always been a destination on campus.

While it has not always been given the most coveted office space on campus, a minority of campuses are finding ways to move the career centers into more high traffic areas in an effort to increase student awareness of the need to take ownership of their careers. It's a great trend and probably worth the effort - if nothing else, it reminds students on a daily basis they should be working on their careers.

However, the Internet and changing student behaviors are opening an opportunity for colleges to begin to put more career services "in the cloud" and to make them accessible on any device, at any time. Students stopped using email when they discovered the instant communication of texting, and later the group communication that Twitter offers, as well as the personal messaging capabilities of Facebook.

With the advanced tools and capabilities that smart phones introduced, students are shifting away from computers and are using their phones to communicate and get the information they need, when they need it.

A study that examined the behaviors of one million users of StudyBlue found that students using a mobile app from their Smartphone spend 40 minutes more studying each week, compared to students who rely solely on a website. According to Becky Splitt, CEO of StudyBlue,

"Mobile studiers take advantage of the downtime they inevitably experience throughout the day. While waiting for coffee or riding the bus home, students are flipping through flashcard decks on their smart phones to efficiently master classroom material and make the most of their valuable time."

Career centers are constantly competing with other campus clubs and activities to gain mind share and time of students. Students today have learned how to multitask and move from one activity to the next with relative ease. Their changing behaviors and the advanced capabilities of SmartPhones and SmartPads is opening an opportunity to deliver career information even more easily.

Studying from their Smartphones enables students to multitask and get in 10-20 minutes of studying here and there throughout the day. Career centers have an enormous opportunity to deliver bite sized learning opportunities to take advantage of these changing behaviors.

To take advantage of these behavior changes, career centers will need to:

- Put more thought into the design of their websites and make them accessible by SmartPhones and SmartPads.

- Include distance learning career courses and tools to create online career plans.

- Utilize social media plug-ins to increase participation.

- Include Badge technology to reward students for participating.

- Adopt crowd sourcing tools to answer questions and increase engagement.

- Use online career fairs to connect students and businesses 24/7/365.

- Build in the ability for parents to be given permission to track students' progress and offer suggestions about how they can keep things on track.

- Create reports that will track students' progress in building their career strategies.

Taking the career center to the clouds will be one of the most critical requirements of building excitement about career management for students.

To start providing entry level career services in the Cloud, get together with your team and:

1. Identify which of your services can be transferred to the Cloud.

1. Evaluate your website and determine if you can make it accessible via SmartPhones and SmartPads.

1. Determine the budget requirements and share those with management.

This is probably one of the more important strategies to increase the amount of time students invest in career exploration, career planning and learning job search skills. Your career center is already behind in this area. Remind your management how drastically technology has changed the behaviors of your students and how you have a unique opportunity to encourage them to take ownership of their careers by being where they are, anytime, through any device.

GET PARENTS TO WORK FOR YOUR CAREER CENTER

Parents have a vested interest in their student's career

According to the Career Advisory Board's report Counseling Graduating Students, 34.1 percent of career professionals rated their number one problem is getting students to use the career center resources.

If nearly 61 percent of graduating seniors either never visit the career center, or visit less than two times, one can only imagine how few freshmen, sophomores and juniors utilize the services provided by the career center. With only an hour or two spent at the career center, it's literally impossible for students to pick up the knowledge they need to get a job.

In that brief time seniors will need to learn how to develop professional networks, use social media in their job searches, pick up interviewing techniques, learn how to search for a jobs, and of course create professional resumes.

Because the college cannot, and will not in the foreseeable future, put in place requirements for students to invest time and effort in exploring career options, and learning job search skills and techniques, in my opinion, it will be up to parents to require their students to start working on their career plans the minute those students arrive on campus. That is, unless the government takes action and requires colleges to ramp up career service requirements to their students...and we shouldn't be surprised when they do. In the summer of 2011, Congress passed legislation that now requires for profit colleges to show that their students' degrees will result in jobs that are related to the degrees and pay enough to offset their student loan payments. The "Gainful Employment" legislation in some form will be imposed on non-profit colleges, too!

Get ahead of students', parents' and legislatures' expectations.

There is evidence that students lean on their parents for career guidance and help in their job searches. The Career Advisory Board's research showed that 76.6 percent of the students surveyed indicated their parents were a valuable resource to help them in their job searches.

Career centers should consider developing a program that:

1. Communicates to parents the issues their students face if they don't take ownership of their careers their freshman years and share stats and research that show the benefits of students utilizing career center resources.

2. Asks parents to require their students to develop career plans and require their students to use the career center facilities.

TalentMarks has developed a CareerParents program that provides the parents of incoming freshman a copy of the ebook, The Employed Grad, Knowledge, Skills and Tools Your Student Will Need to Get a Job, as well as a branded CareerParent portal that gives parents access to videos, webinars featuring career authors, coaches, hiring managers and even grads that regret not building career strategies prior to graduation.

There are other benefits of engaging incoming freshmen parents. First, the college will be able to brag to prospective students' parents about the program. Second, satisfied parents will be more inclined to contribute to the parents' fund when asked. Third, if a grad is unemployed by graduation day, the parent will be less likely to blame the career center or college who offered solutions and strategies four years earlier.

Every student that fails to take ownership of his or her career during freshman year will inevitably find themselves working harder to find a job that is related to his or her major at graduation. In a survey conducted by the Associated Press, students who did not have a job by graduation day would:

"more likely work as waiters, waitresses, bartenders and food-service helpers than as engineers, physicists, chemists and mathematicians combined."

So how do you get started developing a program to engage parents?

1. Meet with your team to determine what you want to accomplish with your career parent program.

2. Develop the curriculum, email communications, e-newsletters, and/or webinars that will help them understand their role.

3. Start your program with the next incoming freshman class and work through the bugs during the year.

I'm convinced this is the fastest, least expensive and least labor intensive strategy, designed to increase the number of students who take ownership of their careers. Parents have a huge stake in this game. You need their help and you will find parents are ready, willing and able to help.

3 REASONS TO START A CAMPUS CAREER CLUB

Campus career clubs will give you more resources, engage more students and raise the awareness of careers on campus.

How many clubs do you have on campus?

It's not unusual for a campus to have anywhere from 30 to 300 clubs and organizations students can join. There are sport clubs, like flag football, ping pong, sailing club and soccer as well as skiing, Chess, Young Republicans, Young Democrats and more.

So why not a Career Club?

I spent a half hour searching the web to see if I could find some colleges that have career clubs, but I had a hard time finding relevant examples. I found a career club Facebook page for a Puerto Rican college, and the rest were community clubs, or K-12 clubs that were named "Job Clubs".

This exercise got me thinking about the benefits of developing a Campus Career Club. Let's do a little brainstorming and kick around some of the benefits of starting a Campus Career Club!

1) It's all about money and resources!

By starting a Career Club, you will qualify for funds you can use to further your department goals. Every organization on campus receives operating funds for events activities and supplies. This could be another

133

way for you to have funds available to invite speakers, hold workshops and continue to add new resources to prepare grads for their first professional job searches.

2) You get another opportunity to engage students!

One of the things I encouraged each of my kids to do as they entered college, was to join clubs and organizations that interested them. As an employer of recent grads, I have always looked at the activities the prospective employee was involved in. A student that had a leadership position within the clubs and organizations he or she belonged to usually got a second look. A Career Club will give students another opportunity to take leadership positions, while at the time giving them experience in managing people.

3) You have another opportunity to get the campus focused on careers.

The Higher Education Research Institution at UCLA has produced the CIRPS Freshman study for the past 3 decades. In their survey of 2013 freshman, they reported that 88 percent of freshman are going to college to improve their chances for careers. (That's up 20% in the past 2 decades) I would use this report to confirm to management the need to start a Career Club.

A Career Club will give you additional opportunities to engage alumni and business leaders as well as take field trips with students to companies' headquarters. After a while you will be able to share stats showing students who are members of the Career Club not only get internships and jobs relevant to their majors, but jobs at higher pay.

How would you structure your club?

That should be the easy part. You probably have a department on campus that coordinates clubs. They should be able to give you a form that will help guide you in developing your club's vision, mission and goals, as well as the fundamentals of what the club will do.

I would encourage you to find a primary focus. Don't duplicate the services or activities of your career center. I would use the Career Club to encourage students to visit the career center, but I wouldn't use it to offer workshops on resumes etc.

You might want to have your Campus Career Club focus on:

1. <u>Soft skills</u>. Companies have been moaning for decades that grads don't have leadership, ethics, communication, teamwork and related skills. Your club could deliver these type of skills to members.

2. Another direction for your club might be to focus more on <u>career exploration</u>. The club might be focused on giving students more focus on how to evaluate industries, companies, and positions for which they would qualify.

3. Yet another direction for your club might be to bring students <u>together with hiring authorities, department managers and others in Google Hangouts</u>, to ask questions and gain wisdom from their experiences.

4. Or, you might focus on taking <u>field trips to companies</u>. The Ski Club travels to the slopes, so why not a monthly visit to a local company for tours and discussions with management combined with a follow-up report or assignment?

Does that make sense? The idea is not to duplicate a service or activities your college currently offers but to find a niche in which you'd like students to get more exposure and experience.

While I know you already have a lot on your plate, I suggest you make sure your club has a number of leadership positions that can be responsible for meetings, scheduling events, handling correspondence with members and briefing you on results. More than likely you will want to have traditional club positions. President, VP, Secretary, Membership, etc. The more, the better-- not only to spread the work around-- but as I mentioned to give students the opportunity to put their leadership roles on their resumes.

PROVEN WAY TO HELP MORE GRADS PREPARE FOR JOB SEARCH

You are missing out on an amazing new service that helps prepare grads for their first professional job searches!

You are probably aware of the stat provided by the Department of Labor that suggests the average young learner will have between 11-14 jobs by the time he or she is 38 years old.

I wonder if your administration is aware of that.

You know better than I that a large percentage of your grads are not prepared for their first professional job searches. Worse, they are not prepared for the subsequent 10 to 13 job searches.

As you know it takes a good deal of time and effort to secure a job. Tony Beshara author of the book, <u>The Job Search Solution</u>, and President of Babich Associates, a professional executive placement firm, who has personally placed 8,000 people in jobs during his 30 year career, suggests it will take an average of 16 interviews for most to get jobs. Leading up to those interviews, job seekers have to spend dozens, if not hundreds of hours developing their resumes, networking, and executing job searches.

For most people the job search process ranks right up there with dealing with the death of a close friend or family member. For even more, the job search process brings a significant amount of anxiety, uncertainty and doubt. Even the highest achievers will have their confidence knocked around during their job search processes.

When you think about it, it's a pretty sad fact that the NUMBER ONE skill your graduates will need during their lives–the number one skill that will help them lead successful lives– is the one the college administration supports the least.

Without proper skills and knowledge, it's safe to say at least 50% of your grads will struggle through the job search process.

It doesn't have to be that way. There is a solution.

TalentMarks now offers a way you can provide grads and alumni access to career programming 24/7 through any device.

Better yet, the program does not require any time of your staff.

The program grew out of the webinar series TalentMarks provided to over 1,000 career centers from the fall of 2010 through the spring of 2013. The series brought 18 top career authors via webinars to the career centers and students. The 200,000 students that took advantage of these webinars picked up incredible tips, best practices and innovative strategies.

It was from this experience that TalentMarks developed the CareerWebinars for Alumni & Students.

Here's how the program would work for you:

TalentMarks will create for your college a branded Career Portal that will includes:

- 18 live and recorded webinars featuring the nation's top career authors.

- Access to 24 incredible career tools to help grads get noticed.

- Daily updates from top career bloggers and news sources.

- A discussion area to kick around career ideas with others.

- A customizable career plan that will offer suggestions based on what skills or knowledge your students and grads need

Plus, the Career Portal provides analytics that will show which alumni and students are participating. It's an innovative idea that has caught fire.

TalentMarks makes it easy for you.

They host, manage and handle all aspects of holding live webinars and then update your portal with the recordings after the webinars. They even handle customer service issues, login problems and regular maintenance of the website.
Plus, they provide marketing materials to promote the program. You receive:

- Copy and graphics to promote each speaker

- Flyers and post cards to share with students and grads

The program is hard to resist!

...and as a result has been enormously popular.

In just the last 12 months, nearly 150 colleges have signed up for the service. We have some colleges that already have over 2000 alumni and grads participating. It's obvious there is a need for the service!

You might consider partnering with your alumni office on this program.

The alumni office is always looking for ways to engage students and young alumni. This is an ideal way you can introduce the alumni association to students and grads. It's another way you can build relationships that provide valuable services to them when they need it most, and it's a simple way to connect with alumni and students as they connect with one another.

The development office benefits, too.

Richard Bolles, author of the bestselling career book, What Color is Your Parachute, once said, "A working alum, is a giving alum!"

PERFORMANCE BASED FUNDING - WHAT YOUR CAREER CENTER NEEDS TO KNOW!

States are adopting funding programs to encourage universities to graduate MORE students!

This is a good news article. Your career center is about to become the most popular department on campus!

While the primary focus of this article is for state supported universities, private college career center professionals can still use the information to share with management so collectively you can develop and implement strategies your college will need to not only remain competitive, but meet the expectations of your prospective students and their families!

I've been watching my alerts and news feeds the past year and I'm starting to see a huge uptick in state and federal administrators talking about the need to switch higher education funding formulas from focusing on enrollment to the number of students graduated.

It's making most higher education administrators nervous! With only 1 out of 2 students actually finishing college, even the discussion of a formula change would make any administrator worried! However, in the states I've been following including my own (Ohio), the legislatures, and governors are inviting university administrators to the table and giving them a huge voice in how the funding formulas are being designed and implemented. I'm getting the impression that universities are being given some ramp up time to develop strategies and implement new ideas to increase graduation rates before they affect their funding.

You hold one of the keys to increasing the graduation rate!

You are probably wondering why legislatures are doing this! If you believe industry experts, based on the current graduation rate, our country will have 3,000,000 less graduates than are needed by 2018. I'm somewhat suspect of this claim when we face the reality of today!

• The Associated Press surveys last year showed approximately 1.5 million, or 53% of graduates 25 or younger are either unemployed or underemployed.

• The fact is that we still have 8 million underemployed, experienced workers as a result of the 2008 downturn, and another 3 million or so that have dropped out of the workforce because they couldn't find work.

Be that as it may, states are also moving to this strategy because research conducted by the CEOs for Cities organization cities a higher percentage of graduates who are not only economically better off, but that the average citizen earns more too! With that extra money circulating through the economy, small businesses benefit, which results in higher sales taxes collected. <u>I'm sure legislatures like the idea that a worker with a degree will also pay higher state taxes!</u>

So that's probably the REAL reason!

There is preliminary evidence that performance based funding does works. Although the effects of an entirely performance-based funding formula are unknown, there is some evidence that it can tip the numbers in the direction of a higher graduation rate. In Pennsylvania, four-year institutions have received performance-based funding for the last decade. During that time, graduation rates have increased by about 10 percentage points, and retention rates for Hispanic students have increased by 15 percentage points.

Because of this, twelve states, Illinois, Indiana, Louisiana, Michigan, Minnesota, New Mexico, Ohio, Oklahoma, Pennsylvania, South Dakota, Tennessee and Washington, have already implemented this strategy.

Most are tip toeing into the program by setting aside 5%-25% of their higher education funding, but one state, Tennessee, has completely changed gears and is funding 100% of higher education based on their universities' graduation rates. Another dozen states like North Carolina are following the legislatures and Governors in the above states and having formal discussions, and or sub-committees working out their formula. The bottom line is this. <u>This idea is sweeping the nation FASTER than anything in the history of higher education legislation and your college/university better be prepared!</u>

Now the great news for you is that you can position your career center at the very center of this new strategy.

The latest research by UCLA's Higher Education Research Institute (HERI) indicates that 88 percent of incoming freshman are going to college because they believe it will help their careers and result in higher lifetime earnings. <u>You could use this research to remind those you report to that this indicates students would invest more time in career exploration, planning and management if only they were required to.</u>

I mentioned earlier in this book about Campus Compact. Campus Compact requires their members to have their presidents sign a compact that that requires the college's graduates to put in a minimum of number of hours in community service or volunteer work before they graduate. While I think this is a noble idea, however, as we discussed already students are NOT going to college to become better citizens - THEY WANT JOBS!

Instead of volunteer time require "career management" time

Knowing that an organization like this exists could help you get your president on board to support a requirement that students invest time in career management.

You already have research you can pull from NACE that shows students that invest more time at the career centers not only get internships and jobs, but also get jobs and at higher salaries.

But don't sit back and wait for your managers to talk about this.

You need to be at the front end of these discussions. Your department is a strategic player in helping the college/university craft a successful strategy to increase the graduation rate.

It's your opportunity to raise awareness about your department's need for more:

- Staffing

- Resources

- Funding

...and be sure to emphasize the positive effect it will make on the graduation rate, enrollment rate and bonus funding provided under these new funding formulas!

HOW DO YOUR STUDENTS, GRADS & ALUMNI RATE YOUR CAREER CENTER?

Students feedback will help you INCREASE funding and staffing

About a decade ago, I was speaking at the Council for Advancement and Support for Education conference in Great Britain on the effectiveness of alumni online communities, when I met Jim Black, President of SEMworks. Jim was at the same conference speaking about the benefits of creating a culture on campus that focused on student satisfaction.

Jim works with admissions and student affairs offices auditing their procedures and processes and offers suggestions to improve systems to increase enrollment, retention and student satisfaction. He's in high demand by institutions who are building successful and sustainable recruiting strategies.

In reviewing some of Jim's white papers recently, I started to wonder if his principals could be applied to career services. It got me asking:

- Are career centers focused on continual improvement?

- Are students, graduates and alumni satisfied with the career centers' services?

- Could career centers reorganize themselves to be more relevant to students, grads and alumni in an employment market that has dramatically changed since 2008?

I realized I couldn't answer these questions, because I haven't been privy to polls from individual colleges that could answer them. Over the years, I've been impressed with the surveys and data provided by NACE to help career professionals benchmark their industry salaries, staffing, student engagement, employment and budgets. The information has been helpful for organizations to determine if they are keeping pace with peer institutions.

What the surveys don't do however, is give career centers a view of how effective their departments are at providing the services students/grads and alumni want, nor do they capture their overall satisfaction.

It got me thinking about the types of questions your career center could ask students and grads. While not a complete list, here are some questions I came up with while listening to an Enya music channel on Pandora!

1. What is the number one outcome your students expect of your service?

2. How do students rate your overall service?

3. How would they rate your department on:

    - Helping them evaluate career opportunities?

    - Teaching them to build career plans?

    - Showing them job search skills?

    - Connecting them with alumni?

    - Preparing them for interviews?

    - Helping them get jobs?

    - Resources you provide?

4. Would they likely recommend your services to fellow students?

5. Which of your services do students think needs to be improved?

6. What hours of operation would your students like you to be open?

7. What new services would your students like you to provide?

8. Which service do they rate as providing them the least value? Best value? Why?

9. What do students say keeps them from using more of your services?

10. How do they rate your services and availability post-graduation?

If you are doing a survey of your students, consider talking to students ahead of time and even holding a focus group to learn what questions you should be asking them. Your survey may not ask the right questions if you don't listen to your customers first!

Don't be afraid of the results!

It's no secret that you are short staffed, that you have a limited, if not diminishing budget and that your college administration is not focused on your department. Properly done, your survey will show why your department needs more resources!

I don't want you focusing ONLY on sugar-coated questions designed to make your department look good!

Your survey should include tough questions. In my opinion your goal in doing the survey is to show the administration what your customers are expecting of you. You can use this opportunity to show the administration that your hands are tied to improve customer satisfaction until you get the right resources.

I specifically listed the first question because you and I know what the answer is without polling your students. Your students expect that your services will help them secure a job!

So if your students, who belong to a generation who are mortgaging their future by attending your college, expect you to help them get a job, why don't you explore ways to help more of them get internships and have jobs by graduation day?

• If they indicate the hours you are open are inconvenient for them, why not explore ways you can be open on evenings, weekends, or provide 24/7 career advice and help?

- If your resume advice is not rated 5 stars, why not come up with ways you can make it five-star including offering online resources and even a course on resume development?

- If they indicate they need more help in basic skills after they graduated, why not develop strategies to provide "distance education" career services and coaching after they graduate?

In an era when you are being asked to take budget and staffing cuts - instead of being a "good soldier" and accepting the cuts - consider using surveys to show how short changing your department in resources will result in:

- More students dropping out of college.

- Fewer grads having a job by graduation day.

- Alumni having less successful careers - which result in less contributions!

<u>You have an incredible opportunity to change the lives of your students and grads.</u>

We are standing at the cross roads where the political climate, economic environment, students' and parents' demands - will FORCE colleges to do more to help students prepare for their careers.

You can either be pushed to come up with strategies that will satisfy your customers' demands or, you can lead the way and build successful strategies which will literally transform lives, and build successful careers!

Which will it be on your campus?

HELP ALUMNI BUILD SUCCESSFUL CAREERS

Study indicates alumni want help in the transitions of their lives!

About 10 years ago, a firm founded by professors from Harvard and Penn State, the Olson Zaltman Associates, was commissioned by the American Insurance Association (now called USI Affinity) and NEATrust to help alumni associations better understand the existing relationship between colleges and their graduates.

The professors had developed an interview technique that gained deep seated insight from subjects by having them select 6 to 8 photographs from which the professors would ask them to describe their current and desired relationship with their alma maters.

Alumni associations that participated in the research were interested in gaining this insight so they could build stronger relationships and engagement with alumni in the future.

The findings of the research were somewhat predictable.

Alumni felt that the alumni association's sole purpose was to raise money for the college. They cited mail, emails, phone calls and events from the alumni association focused on fundraising. They shared that this constant "ask" was rarely balanced with offers to help them.

The study suggests that the transformation from college to career will set the stage on how alumni will view the college for decades to come. If the first contact from the college after graduation is a fundraising request, it will essentially cast in stone the prevailing attitude that the alumni association is only interested in getting money from the graduate.

It also suggested that alumni will be more likely "give back" to their universities when they feel there have been fair exchanges.

But what is a fair exchange?

The next question alumni professionals needed answered was, "What can we offer alumni they would consider as fair exchanges?" The study showed that alumni viewed their college experience as a transformative stage in the journeys of lives. This was followed by their first jobs, careers, marriages, families, finances, empty nesting, and eventually retirement. The research indicated alumni wanted the alumni association to help them in the transitions in their lives.

The firm suggested that alumni associations use this information and find a way they could provide information and guidance and help alumni as they passed through each of these phases. Alumni indicated they would value this information as they have a high degree of trust in the information the college provided them in their undergraduate years.

Alumni associations were advised to gain a better understanding about how they could:

1. Help with the transformation from student to alumni.

2. Be helpful to alumni on their journeys in life.

3. Provide valuable information and resources to alumni.

Let's look at the first suggestion! The easiest place for alumni associations to start implementing these strategies is with helping students migrate from campus to their first professional jobs.

In my blog posts, I frequently share a survey of nearly 600 college career directors conducted by the Career Advisory Board that suggests:

*   48.1% thought students did not have the knowledge they needed to find jobs.

- 55.7% felt students resumes were not professional enough to use for their job searches.

It's no secret that few students take ownership of their careers while in college. A NACE survey found that during their senior years, over 61 percent of graduating students either never visited the career center, or visited only once, or twice. It's no wonder that career center professionals cite the above issues.

The good news is that this represents a tremendous opportunity for the alumni association to step in and provide career networking and training. A number of new opportunities are becoming available to help.

A growing number of alumni associations are adding staff to focus in this area and others are working more closely with their career centers to help them develop programs focused on the needs of working alumni. Now entering their 8th year, the Alumni Career Services Network is a rapidly growing group of dedicated alumni career services professionals who are reaching out to their alumni to provide career assistance. I urge you to join this valuable group and support their cause!

What are you thinking of doing to help your alumni?

"If opportunity doesn't knock, build a door."

- Milton Burle

6 THE REALITIES YOUR GRADS FACE

Now let's take a detailed look at the issues your students and graduates are facing.

The following mini-chapters are designed to draw attention to the additional hurdles Millennials face when compared to other generations. I don't need to tell you that things are different today. You are in the trenches and see more on a daily basis then I see in a year. The key to making things better for your graduates is to get management to rally around your strategies and ideas and put the full weight of the administration behind you.

In the preceding chapter, we discussed a number of ideas. Now, we need to make sure management understands that things are very different for today's grads. We need to make sure they understand the college has to focus on becoming a career centered college campus or risk losing enrollment, contributions and a stellar reputation.

The following discussion is designed to give you solid arguments that will encourage management to formulate changes in policy, processes, and funding.

The first discussion is one of the most important to share with management as it clearly lays out the cost of not giving your grads the skills to get a job. It's a simple idea. If the average grad takes 7.4 months to find a job, then the college needs to do whatever it takes to help all grads land a job by graduation day. Each month you shave off of that national average puts $3,000 to $4,000 in each grad's pocket.

The last discussion, *What Does Your College Owe Graduates?* is designed to start a discussion about identifying what the college could be doing differently to solve some of the issues and problems facing grads today.

I know--just by looking at the title-- this section is kind of a downer, but it's about the realities your grads face today.

They don't have to be facing these issues.

You've got ideas to solve them. Use the stats, facts and concepts in this section to shock management into action.

Have management put themselves in the shoes of your grads!

Here are the 9 topics we'll discuss:

1. Your Class of 2013 Will Lose $12,000,000 in Wages

2. 8 Ways Organizations are "Waging War" on Students & Grads!

3. Students and Parents put Too Much Focus On Getting Into College

4. 5 Reasons Graduates Do Not Get Jobs!

5. The Quick Death of College Internships

6. New Grad Employability Exam

7. Why Can't Johnny Find a Job?

8. When Will Parents and Students Revolt?

9. What Does Your College Owe Graduates?

YOUR CLASS OF 2014 WILL LOSE $12,000,000 IN WAGES

If your grads had job by graduation day they could pay off their student loans!

If your college graduates 500 students, your Class of 2014 will collectively lose $12,000,000 in wages because they won't have a job by graduation day.

How did I come up with that?

The National Association of Colleges and Employers 2011 Student Benchmark study showed that the average grad took 7.4 months to get a job after graduation. Assuming the average grad earns $3,000 per month, the average grad lost nearly $24,000 in salary because he or she did not have a job lined up immediately after graduation. Now take the lost salary for one grad, and multiply that by 500, and you get $12,000,000! That's the cumulative lost salary of all grads. Think that is a huge chunk of change? Consider these numbers!

- 1,000 grads results in $24,000,000 of lost salary

- 2,000 grads results in $48,000,000 of lost salary

- 4,000 grads results in $96,000,000 of lost salary

A large state college would see its Class of 2014 lose out on earning $100,000,000! The 1,700,000 students that graduate nationwide will collectively lose out on earning $40,800,000,000! Yep that's BILLIONS!

Is anyone taking responsibility to drive this number down?

This is such a HUGE, mind numbing number that I would think the president's council at colleges; banks, Sallie Mae, the government, or somebody would be doing something to help grads line up jobs by graduation day.

But sadly I'm not seeing any significant movement, plan or program being introduced. I was hoping the Occupy Wall Street Movement would spill over to college campuses and that students would raise their concerns about this to administrators. But it didn't. I was hoping parents would start shopping for colleges based on the successful job search stats of their grads. But it hasn't happened. I know career center professionals like yourself have been trying to get the administration to provide more resources, to require students take career courses, but all you've gotten is budget cuts!

I know from surveys, like the one conducted by the Career Advisory Board, career center professionals like yourself are very concerned that you can't effectively help grads because students have a poor understanding of the effort required to secure employment.

So what could be done to reduce the number of months it takes a grad to get a job? The Department of Labor reminds us there are 3,000,000 jobs available at any one time. Could your campus adopt strategies to make sure your grads grabbed these by the time they graduated? I think so. Here are a few ideas that don't require a lot of money, time, permission and/or resources!

1. Administrators need to focus the campus culture on careers.

2. Students should be required to invest time in career planning.

3. The government needs to provide tax incentives to firms hiring grads.

4. Parents need to keep their students focused on careers.

5. The alumni association needs to actively connect students and alumni.

1) Administrators need to focus the campus culture on careers.

A yearly study by the UCLA's Higher Education Research Institute shows that 88 percent of the 2013 incoming freshman are going to college in order to improve their odds of getting jobs and having successful careers.

If that is the case, why are we not emphasizing careers instead of sports, 400 clubs, and volunteerism? The career center is near the bottom of the list when you compare the budget per student served, or career advisor to student ratio. This will require the administration to get the faculty behind your plan to require students to take career courses and encourage them to incorporate in the curriculum an understanding of how the student will be able to use the information learned in seeking a career.

2) Students should be required to invest time in career planning.

I mentioned in my book, The Unemployed Grad, And What Parents Can Do About It, an organization called the Campus Compact where 1200 college presidents committed their colleges to require students to invest a specific number of hours volunteering in community service events, but NONE required student to invest time in career planning.

If students were required their freshman year to follow a curriculum that includes networking with alumni, researching industries, companies and jobs, and building their job search strategies, they would more likely have had internships and jobs lined up by graduation day. Consider adding a required four year curriculum and career planning methodology your students can follow. Consider including online career courses, presentations by career experts, webinars and resources.

3) The government needs to provide tax incentives to firms hiring grads.

We have our third child in college and I've been very thankful for the American Opportunity Tax Credit as it offers $2,500 credit for sending our daughter to college. When a student is sitting home on the couch, he or she is not earning a salary that could be taxed. Further the grad is holding off on purchases that would result in sales tax collected by states. Not having a job is also depressing the economy because parents are probably funneling money to help their grads pay for entertainment, money that could have found its way in purchases, family vacations or splurges on new household items.

So why can't state and federal governments come together and offer a $5,000 package to companies who hire grads within 30 days of graduation?   I'm no tax expert but let's assume the student's $3,000 salary had a 10 percent federal tax assessment and another 7 percent for state taxes.   In 8 months, the government would have earned the $2,500 tax credit from the student. The state would recoup the money by the end of the year.

4) Parents need to keep their students focused on careers.

Assuming the college can't require students to invest time in their careers, the next option is to get parents to require their sons or daughters to take ownership in their careers. Parents have for decades assumed the college was investing time in their sons or daughters and giving them the skills they needed to get jobs. As you know that's not the case.

With so much time and money invested in their students, parents are natural partners to engage and take some of the responsibility of getting their kids nudged in the right directions. We created the CareerParents Online Community to help colleges do that. The program provides a branded website where parents can download a copy of the book, The Employed Grad, Knowledge, Skills and Information Your Grad Needs To Get a Job, as well as related videos, webinars and even a discussion area. We believe this is the fastest way to bring institutional change and set the stage for grads who are focused on having a job by graduation day.

5) The alumni association needs to actively connect students and alumni.

This whole situation could be eliminated if alumni stepped up to the plate and agreed to hire a student in their firm and colleges offered the firm $2,500 to hire the grad. Assuming 200 out of the 500 grads are hired by alumni this way, the college would be committing $500,000 a year to the project. This effort would go a long way to show recent grads that the college is committed to helping them get jobs after they graduate. It's also a great recruiting tool.

Let's assume you don't like that idea and you take another direction. I'm going to assume you have 40,000 alumni if you are graduating 500 students a year. Development officers talk about how alumni give of their Time, Treasure or Talents. In this case we are we'd reach out to alumni to use their talents. In an upcoming chapter I'll detail how your annual giving office can reach out to alumni in the spring with a Mentoring Campaign. The idea is to use the annual giving calling team to call alumni to ask them to mentor students. The team would call alumni and get a commitment from the caller and then match them with a student. The campaign would be designed to match every freshman student with a mentor. During that call you could also ask them to help a grad get a job. They could be matched with a senior with the same major or interests.

Conclusion

So we talked about 5 ways to reduce the number of months it takes a grad to find a job. Each individually could help--collectively all five, plus other initiatives you are thinking about, will vastly decrease the time it takes a grad to get a job after he or she graduate.

In the end, everyone wins!

1. Students get jobs, and pay off their loans quicker.

2. States keep students working in their state, paying taxes.

3. Businesses increase revenue from more money flowing.

4. Colleges will increase enrollment because parents will want their kids to go to colleges committed to help with employment.

Let's decrease the time it takes for a grad to get a job. Help us increase awareness by sharing this post with others.

8 WAYS ORGANIZATIONS ARE "WAGING WAR" ON STUDENTS & GRADS!

*Legislative policies, banks, and even your college is making life
difficult for students and grads*

During the last presidential election I kept hearing about a "War on Women." The term initially shocked me, and caught my attention.

"Could there really be a war on woman? What is it? How is it affecting woman? Who is waging it? Should I get involved?"

Examples cited by politicians and repeated by the media included legislation restricting contraception; cutting off funding for Planned Parenthood; medically unnecessary ultrasounds; abortion taxes; abortion waiting periods; forcing women to tell their employers why they want birth control, and prohibiting insurance companies from including abortion coverage in their policies.

The discussion dominated the airwaves for months and raised important issues that forced candidates to step out from behind their sound bites and share their opinions.

So it got me thinking...

Since 2008, the employment market has tanked for college grads. There are half dozen studies that show millennial grads are facing issues that previous generations did not.

- They carry more debt.

- They face a tighter, more competitive job market that is hiring fewer and fewer grads.

- They are shouldering a higher percentage of their education costs.

- More of them are unemployed, or underemployed.

Yet, nothing is being done to alleviate these issues.

- At the same time, colleges are graduating more students, who need to learn how to search for and to land jobs, while career center budgets are being slashed.

- While the government and other organizations are falling over themselves to provide the one million veterans from the last decade of wars with career counseling, college tuition programs, and job search programs, very LITTLE is being done to help today's graduates.

My Google Reader fills up this time of year with personal stories about students facing these issues. I hear parents grumble, business and organization leaders complain, and legislative leaders offer sound bites, but I don't see any programs being implemented to help recent grads. Everyone bitches about their issues but nothing is being done to help grads!

Is there a War on Students and Grads?

After thinking about this, it occurred to me that maybe there was a concerted effort to take advantage of students and grads...but, is it serious enough that one could label it a "War on Students and Grads"?

If there is such a war, how can we provide evidence to that effect?

First, I realized I had to build a list that would clearly outline why grads are getting short changed in today's economy and who is, or isn't, helping them!

Next, I started thinking about how we could educate the media, congress and the decision makers at our colleges and universities. I started to think about using PR techniques to build a media frenzy around the "War on Students and Grads" theme, so we can marshal the creative energy of the media, parents, students, grads, alumni, hiring authorities, and entrepreneurs to come up with solutions. That led me to thinking about the value of a movement, similar to Occupy Wall Street, that could take on a life of its own and spread quickly across all 50 states.

Any good PR campaign needs a compelling message that the intended audience can relate to and so they are inspired to action. It also needs facts that support its message. To help get the discussion started on what could be included on that list, here are 8 ways our culture and institutions are waging a "War on Students and Grads"!

1. Congress gives Wall Street & banks access to free cash, but wants to double the interest on Stafford student loans.

2. Congress allows businesses and individuals to discharge loans in bankruptcies, but not students.

3. Congress has made it harder for students to get credit cards because they don't think they are responsible enough to handle credit, yet they will trust them to operate 130 million dollar tanks.

4. Congress and the Labor Department look the other way as organizations (some report as high as 50%) do not pay students while they are employed in internships.

5. State legislatures have significantly cut back on funding for higher education, forcing students and their families to take on enormous debt.

6. Congress is doing little to nothing to help grads get jobs.

7. Colleges are doing little to nothing to help grads get jobs.

8. Congress is forcing students to begin paying for health benefits.

Let's take a closer look at how this is affecting students and grads.

1. Congress gives Wall Street & banks access to free cash, but wanted to double the interest on Stafford student loans.

Wall Street and banks can borrow money at as little as 1% and re-lend it at an enormous profit. Today, a home owner with good credit can refinance their mortgage for as little as 2.75%. So why does congress need to make students pay more interest? It's not like they are losing money. According to the Congressional Budget Office, the federal government will make $34 billion off student loans in 2013, a number that will only increase with higher interest rates. Currently, the federal government will make 12.5 cents for every dollar of subsidized loans it gives out, 33.3 cents for every dollar of unsubsidized loans, 54.8 cents for every dollar of graduate student loans and 49 cents for every dollar of parent loans. Why the War on Students and Grads?

2. Congress allows businesses and individuals to discharge loans in bankruptcies, but not students.

In 2005, Congress gave private student loan vendors a gift. They passed a new law that made it impossible for a student to discharge his or her student loans in bankruptcy. This happened just a few years before the economy tanked, enrollment of out-of-work students soared, and the cost of education zoomed. If a young person wanted to go out and buy an $80,000 home, there is a good chance he or she would not have the 20 percent down payment required, or an income level to support the loan. But virtually any student or immigrant that has been credit-worthy (at least in the past 5 years) can spend $80,000 of borrowed money on a college education. Large companies and Wall Street firms have benefited from bankruptcy at the cost of trillions of dollars. Why the War on Students and Grads?

3. Congress has made it harder for students to get credit cards because they don't think they are responsible enough to handle credit, yet they will trust them to operate 130 million dollar tanks.

A few years back congress passed legislation that controlled how credit card companies could solicit college students. Their concern was that students were racking up way too much debt on their credit cards, and didn't have a way to repay them. In fact, the average grad had $5,000 of credit card debt, ON TOP of his or her student loan debt. But with credit now tightened for new students who are facing higher tuition, book costs and related expenses, where are they going to get the extra money? When banks, Wall Street, and businesses face new legislations, an army of consultants pounce on political leaders and their staffers to wring out concessions and changes in the law-- Why the War on Students and Grads?

4. Congress and the Labor Department look the other way as organizations (some report as high as 50%) do not pay students while they are employed in internships.

Why do some of the nation's top companies, companies that make millions in profit, not pay interns? As internships become an important stepping stone for students to show experience to hiring managers, Internships will continue to be an important experience. Having to accept an unpaid internship forces students further into debt. Students that need internships the most are disadvantaged. Why the War on Students and Grads?

5. State legislatures have significantly cut back on funding for higher education, forcing students and their families to take on enormous debt.

In 2000, student loan debt had barely crossed the $200 billion mark. Today it has increased by five-fold to over $1 trillion dollars. The average graduate of the class of 2013 is reported to have $27,000 in student loan debt. That means he or she will end up committing $300 a month over 10 years to pay back the loan, which will affect his or her ability to buy a car, purchase a home, and start a family. Why the War on Students and Grads?

6. Congress is doing little to nothing to help grads get jobs.

Congress has pulled out all the stops to help the 1,000,000 returning veterans of war, and has the power to offer tax incentives to organizations to hire grads, but they are doing nothing. The unemployment rate for recent college grads in their early 20's is nearly 9%, and when you add in grads that are employed part-time but looking for full time work, and grads that have given up, that number hits 18%. Worse, in the last 12 years, the US has gone from having the highest share of employed 25-34 year-olds among large, wealthy economies to having among the lowest. Wall Street, banks, corporations receive billions of tax benefits -- why can't our best and brightest come up with a way that rewards students for investing their time and money to prepare themselves to make our country self-reliant, safer and more competitive?   Why the War on Students and Grads?

7. Colleges are doing little to nothing to help grads get jobs.

Since 2008, hiring of grads has plummeted. The average grad today takes an average of 7.4 months to get a job, losing out on $24,000 on salary. The associated press shared a survey that showed 53% of grads under 25 were either unemployed or underemployed. The trends do not look good. An NACE survey conducted in the fall of 2012 showed employers anticipated hiring 13% more grads in 2013. Only 6 months later that number was reduced to 2.1%. So what are colleges doing to help? Cutting the career center budget! Why the War on Students and Grads?

8. Congress is forcing students to begin paying for health benefits.

The new health bill will require everyone to get health insurance. I didn't even think about health insurance or start paying for it until I was in my 30's and married. Today, the healthiest that have the least need for health insurance will have to pay for it or hopefully have a parent that has health insurance and can afford to have them on the policy. (It's been reported 40,000,000 people do not have health insurance) So grads will be required to sign up and pay for a portion of their health benefits with the firms that hire them.   Why the War on Students and Grads?

Do you think there is a "War on Students and Grads"?

Can you help start the discussion about the war our culture, organizations and institutions are waging on our students and grads? What can you do to bring attention to the continual burdens our policies are placing on students and grads so that we can give them a decent shot at achieving their dreams and living the kinds of lives they deserve?

STUDENTS AND PARENTS PUT TOO MUCH FOCUS ON GETTING INTO COLLEGE

New career assessment test for your grads

 Students go to college to get a job, but do nothing while in college to learn the skills they need to get a job!

Ask any parents why they want their kid to go to college, and you will hear them unanimously say, "I want my child to be able to get a good job!"

Ask any incoming freshman why he or she is going to college, and you will hear him or her say the same thing. Studies confirm that fact. The Higher Education Research Institution (HERI) at UCLA has produced the CIRPS Freshman study for the past 3 decades. The survey polls hundreds of thousands of freshman each year. In their 2012 survey, 88 percent of incoming freshman indicated they were going to college to improve their chances of having successful careers. (That's up 20% in the past 2 decades.)

However—once students get into college— few invest the time necessary to learn the skills, they need to catapult them into successful careers. Even though online communities likeLinkedIn, Facebook, and others have made it easier than ever to meet alumni, few students use them to reach out to willing, employed alumni for help.

Testing to get into college is the new norm – even though it's not required!

Here's why I think students' and their parents focus too much on getting into college and too little on preparing to get jobs after college.

I was reading an article in the New York Times about the time and effort prospective students invest in preparing for ACT and SAT testing. According to the article:

- 1,666,017 students took the ACT

- 1,664,479 students took the SAT

The article shared an emerging trend that students are now taking both tests and investing a great deal of time and money to take the tests again to improve their scores. The author of the article, Tamar Lewin wrote,

"Of this year's 26,000 applicants to Princeton, 13 percent, or 3,477 students, submitted only ACT scores — up from 2 percent (385 of 17,000 applicants) for fall 2006. And almost 8,000 this year submitted scores from both tests. (SAT & ACT)"

Preparing for the SAT and ACT is a huge investment, both financially and in time. To prepare for the 3 1/2 hour SAT test, students will purchase any of a hundred plus books or courses and invest dozens, if not hundreds, of hours in preparation. Parent pay the $51 test fee, fork over another $30 to $60 for prep books, and some are even willing to spend $400 to $10,000 to help their kids improve their scores.

It's a big business that has changed the behavior of students heading to college.

A culture has developed and changed everyone's behavior!

The SAT and ACT tests can be traced way back to the 1900's when a group of colleges got together to identify deserving students through a shared entrance exam, then called "College Boards". The firm College Board has continued to protect and maintain the accuracy of the SAT (Scholastic Aptitude Test).

As more colleges adopted the shared entrance exam, prospective students started seeking help to improve their scores.

By 1945, American universities began relying on standardized tests to measure students' potentials. Stanley Kaplan started coaching and tutoring students in the basement of his home. Stanley knew he could help students improve their scores and started to expand his tutoring program. By 1975, the Federal Trade Commission concluded that test preparation like that provided by Kaplan helped students raise their test scores and passed legislation to make the admissions process more transparent.

A couple decades later in 1981, John Katzman founded Princeton Review to, "Help students to achieve their aspirations through education."

Why not a Career Assessment Test?

So with all this effort and time going into the college application process, why hasn't the culture on campus focused on giving students the skills to get into their first professional jobs?

If parents, students and administrators want to see graduates head into the business world and lead successful careers, why not test to see if the students have the knowledge the organizations that will hire them want them to have?

Why not require them to take Career Access Tests (CATs) to determine if they are job search ready?

A required or recommended CAT would encourage students to focus on investing time in career development while in college and offer companies proof that the college and student are doing more to prepare for their careers, rather than working only to get degrees.

Who's responsible for this?

Should the CareerBoard that has been providing aptitude testing for over three quarters of a century step in and help colleges and businesses build a standard that will offer proof to parents and their grads are ready for their campus-to-corporate transitions?

5 REASONS GRADUATES DO NOT GET JOBS!

Without a career planning process and methodologies students are lost

I have a Google alert set to deliver articles about unemployed graduates to my inbox .

It's a bit depressing but, every day, Google delivers articles about graduates who have a ton of debt, live with mom and dad, are working minimum wage jobs, and are feeling like their college investment was a waste of time and money.

It got me thinking about why this is happening. Why are grads NOT getting jobs?

From my perspective there are five reasons:

1. Graduates picked the wrong major

2. Graduates have unrealistic expectations

3. Colleges and universities are failing to use their alumni networks and faculties to help

4. Graduates have no clue about how to search for jobs

5. No one (biz, college, government) is doing anything to help!

Of the 28 articles I received today that were published in newspapers, blogs and magazines around the world, the one that caught my eye was an article in the Buckinghamshire Advertiser about Sophie Hewit, a recent graduate from the University of West of England who graduated in June with a degree in Drama. Sophie is one of millions of graduates from universities in China, the United States, Great Britain, Scotland and other countries that 5 months after graduation, still cannot find jobs.

Graduates picked the wrong major

Sophie is an example of the first reason. When Sophie entered college, she had 200 different majors she could choose from, but, because she has had a lifelong interest in drama, it was natural for her to choose it. While I agree that everyone deserves an opportunity to follow their passions and interests, they also deserve to know the percent of previous graduates that:

- Got a job that used the skills and knowledge picked up in the curriculum that qualified them for their degrees,

- What percent received any kind of job,

- How far from graduation day they got those jobs, and

- What the average graduate is getting paid

Consumers like Sophie are making the biggest investment in their lives when they go to college, (in many cases bigger than the cost of home ownership) and few to zero colleges actively share such information with prospective students (or for that matter existing students and a their parents). Colleges and universities should counsel and advise graduates PRIOR to them making decisions on majors of what the likelihood will to get jobs... to the point of requiring them to sign a document acknowledging they received the information. <u>It's the only way they are going to pass the responsibility back to the graduate and not have the graduate come back to them and sue the organization for handing them a diploma that doesn't "work"!</u>

Graduates have unrealistic expectations

Talk to any parent, educator or business professional and you'll hear the same thing. Grads have unrealistic expectations when they graduate. Why is that, and who is responsible for setting their expectations? Their networks are pretty tight...

- Aren't they aware that 80 percent their classmates since 2008 have been unemployed by graduation day?

- Isn't their grapevine, amplified by the viral nature of Facebook, keeping them up to date on the reality of their peers' efforts in getting jobs?

Or, are they getting mixed signals by reading articles like this one published in the Wall Street Journal in October, 2011:

The average salary offer for the most recent crop of graduates was up 6% compared to salaries offered to 2010 graduates, according to a survey by the National Association of Colleges and Employers released Tuesday. For those earning bachelor's degrees, salary offers rose to $51,171 from $48,288 in 2010.

My son graduated from Miami University's, Farmer School of Business with a high grade point, multiple leadership positions, and the distinction of his Capstone group project winning first place out of 20 other groups in his class. So when his only offer was an internship at 12 dollars an hour, he just about hit the floor. With no other offers coming in and his plane about to leave for LA, he took the position. Fortunately for him, the two month internship became a full time position. However, the salary offer was closer to the starting salary of a teacher (with a 9 month contract) and nowhere near salary numbers reported in the media or as shared by national associations. My son's expectations were based on surveys by NACE which suggested business majors salaries for the class of 2011 were up 4.6% to $48,805, and that Business administration/ management positions were up 5.4% to $46,372.

If graduates look at these numbers that are repeated in the Wall Street Journal and about every newspaper from the Topeka Capital Journal to the Huffington Post, it's bound to give them unrealistic expectations, <u>and make them feel pretty deflated when they finally get offers in the 30's!</u>

Colleges and universities are failing to use their alumni networks and faculties to help

The average college has 100 alumni for every new graduate. The tens of thousands --and in many cases hundreds of thousands of alumni --work for thousands of companies. How effectively is the college working with alumni and their companies to place graduates? In my opinion, they are doing so poorly. This is not the career office's fault, it's an overlooked opportunity by management.

Think about this for a minute. Every college has dozens of staff in their alumni, annual giving and development offices. For the most part, each is responsible to reach out to alumni and companies to raise money. A large percentage of revenue gifted from capital campaigns comes from companies.

What if the college put the time and staff on working with alumni and their companies to hire their students? If you had 100 alumni working to help place one graduate, I'm certain they would find a way to help that grad get a job.

Graduates have no clue about how to search for jobs

In a previous post, I share the following five reasons why a graduate does not have a clue about how to search for a job.

1. Students are busy completing their curriculum requirements, and don't have time or feel the pressure to build career and job search strategies

2. The career center is only open during class hours. It's inconvenient and doesn't fit in their schedules

3. Students are not aware of the many services the career center can provide because the career center does not have the time to effectively market to them

4. The college has not put a priority on career education and job search strategies (We'll come back to this one!)

5. Students may have negative, preconceived notions about the quality of services provided by the career center and assume they can pick up the skill sets on their own

For details, read the post, but if you don't have time, my suggestions are that colleges should be requiring students to invest a minimum amount of time in career exploration and job search strategies. To accomplish that, they need to provide the career center more resources and make it less of a destination, but put it in the clouds.

No one is doing anything to help!

I've sat back the past four years thinking that the government, colleges, businesses or alumni associations, or perhaps even the chambers of commerce would step forward and do something to help graduates.

President Obama recently offered some loan repayment relief for graduates, but has done nothing to offer a tax benefit to companies to hire graduates, or any kind of moral/emotional support. In the glory days of 2007 when 60 percent of graduates had jobs and another 15-19 percent went on to grad schools, colleges didn't need to do much. But today, with 80 percent of grads unemployed, and colleges and universities almost unilaterally have decided to CUT THE BUDGET of the career center.

And during that time, with alumni unemployment doubling to the point 1 in 6 unemployed people have bachelor's degrees, what are alumni associations doing to help alumni get jobs?

Holding events designed to enhance alumni's sense of nostalgia to make them more likely to contribute to annual giving and capital campaigns.

Few to none think its part of their mission or responsibility to be a resource to help alumni get jobs.

So what do we do?

Sound off and share your opinions!

In order to help the past four graduating classes, the future graduating classes and all alumni, concerned citizens, your management and organizations will need to put some plans in motion in each of the five areas we discussed.

You could become a fantastic asset to help one or 10,000 grads have successful futures. You've got great ideas and the authority to implement them.

This can't be solved without your help!

5

THE QUICK DEATH OF COLLEGE INTERNSHIPS AS WE KNOW THEM

Court ruling could negatively, or positively affect Internships

It's no secret that internships are an important part of grads getting a head start on their careers.

A new survey by The Chronicle and American Public Media's Marketplace, found that employers valued real world experience, internships and work during college four times more then they did the college's reputation.

Research by NACE shows that in terms of starting salary, there is a financial advantage for students who have internship experiences. The NACE 2010 Student Survey showed students with internships received an average salary of $41,580 versus $34,601 for students who didn't have internships.

It's no wonder the number of students participating in internships has been growing dramatically. A study by Northwestern University showed that in 1992 only 17 percent of graduating students held internships versus 50 percent in 2008!

However, a June 2013 decision by a New York judge could spell the end of Internships as we know them.

Internships take the spotlight at the theaters and in court!

It was a bit ironic that the movie featuring Owen Wilson and Vince Vaughn, two 40 year olds who are vying for a spot in Google's internship program, premiered at the same time a federal judge in New York ruled that Fox Searchlight Pictures violated minimum wage and overtime laws by not paying interns who worked on the production of the 2010 movie "Black Swan."

It turns out that one of the interns that brought suit against Fox Searchlight Pictures was a 42 year old MBA grad from Case Western Reserve University whose intern assignments included preparing documents for purchase orders, handling petty cash, and traveling around to obtain signatures on documents, as well as creating spreadsheets and tracking down missing information in employee personnel files.

Eric Glatt was one of over 100 interns that Fox Searchlight Pictures employed during the filming of the movie that did not receive compensation for their time and work. They were given an opportunity to tell future employers that they had "real world" experience.

I'm not privy why, after all these years, someone like Mr. Glatt decided to challenge the system, but he did. Perhaps Mr. Glatt, a keen accountant realized that a movie that took only $13 million dollars to make, then grossed over $300 million, could have afforded to pay him and his colleagues even minimum wage.

Whatever the reason, Eric threw down a gauntlet that has Hollywood, board rooms, colleges, and non-profits quaking. Quaking, because nearly all past interns could be invited by a TV ad to join a class action suit to sue the companies for which they interned. I really don't see students moving on this, but suspect out of work lawyers will see this as a way to right a system that has been "enslaving" college students for decades. In fact, don't be surprised if marketing organizations for attorneys call your office and ask you to post information or <u>share information with students about a class action suit in which they could participate AND even offer a percentage of whatever they win from settlements.</u>

What does the government consider an internship?

In the true spirit of an internship, the internship is all about the student. The internship should be designed around advancing the student's knowledge and experience and not designed to benefit the company or organization for which the student works. That means the student should NOT be doing work that the company would normally hire people to do.

Under federal law, every employee in America is entitled to a minimum wage, additional compensation for overtime, and certain other benefits. In 1947, in the case of Walling v. Portland Terminal Co., the United States Supreme Court held that an organization does not have to provide compensation for labor <u>for people who work for their personal advantages rather than that of their employers.</u> The court looked at this person as a trainee instead of an employee, and offered six factors in which organizations could determine if their internship were for the intern's own educational benefit or the advantages of their employers.

The six factors include:

1. The internship, even though it includes actual operation of the facilities of the employer, is similar to training which would be given in an educational environment.

2. The internship experience is for the benefit of the intern.

3. The intern does not displace regular employees, but works under close supervision of existing staff.

4. The employer that provides the training derives no immediate advantage from the activities of the intern; and on occasion its operations may actually be impeded.

5. The intern is not necessarily entitled to a job at the conclusion of the internship.

6. The employer and the intern understand that the intern is not entitled to wages for the time spent in the internship.

Nearly all internships are loosely put together by companies who believe they are doing a student a favor by providing them a desk, computer and opportunity to handle day to day low risk assignments, like another student who joined Eric in the lawsuit against Fox Searchlight Pictures.

The other plaintiff, Alex Footman, a 2009 Wesleyan graduate who majored in film studies, said his responsibilities included preparing coffee for the production office, ensuring that the coffee pot was full, taking and distributing lunch orders for the production staff, taking out the trash and cleaning the office. You decide. Did any of his responsibilities comply with the above six points?

The judge didn't think so!

The judge, William Pauley III of the U.S. District Court for the Southern District of New York ruled that Fox Searchlight Picture's use of interns in producing the movies "Black Swan" and "(500) Days of Summer" violated minimum-wage and overtime laws, and that the interns can file a class-action lawsuit against the studio. Their activities as I described them above were clearly designed to benefit the organization and not the students.

As a result of this ruling, Nancy J. Leppink, the acting director of the Department of Labor's, wage and hour division warns business leaders,

" If you're a for-profit employer or you want to pursue an internship with a for-profit employer, there aren't going to be many circumstances where you can have an internship and not be paid and still be in compliance with the law."

Wow, after reading that I started to realize that very few internships are designed with this in mind. In fact, the Department Of Labor has taken the position that for the exemption to apply, all of the factors listed above must be met.

So what does that mean for organizations offering internships?

According to Ross Perlin, author of the book, Internation, there are estimated to be about 1.5 million internships in the United States. Of all internships, according to InternBridge, as many as 1/2 are unpaid. Ross Eisenbrey, vice president of the Economic Policy Institute, a liberal-leaning think tank suggests there are a million UNPAID internships alone!

At any rate, how many companies do you think have designed their internships to the guidelines described above?

Not many!

We'll always have internships like Google's that will attract Owen Wilsons and Vince Vaughns because they pay $6,000 per month, but it looks to me that after this ruling, the1/2 million unpaid internships are at risk of being terminated.

After all, what organization wants to be subject to a class action suit of their interns?

I can hear HR departments across the land getting memos from their management offices suggesting they not put the firm in the public relations position that Fox Searchlight Pictures is in, let alone in the legal fix.

There could be a silver lining to all this.

In a perfect world, every organization that offers internships would simply take the easy way out and just pay the interns! However, that will not be so easy for some organizations. The National Association of Colleges and Employers found that 55 percent of the class of 2012 had an internship or co-op during their time in college and almost half of those - 47 percent - were unpaid. Of those, one third of internships at for-profit companies were unpaid.

In tough economic times its not only difficult for companies to part with their cash, but its even more difficult for non-profits!

Regardless, we've got to put our heads together and find a way out of this mess.

If suddenly 30 percent of 1.5 million internships disappear, that means 450,000 students will lose the opportunity to put one on their resumes and they need that treasured word, "internship." It also means those students will lose out on the benefits provided by internships, namely jobs after they graduate--jobs at a higher pay grade.

Organizations, who already say they are having a difficult time finding the right grads to fill their positions will find it even tougher to bring on students who had real world experience during their internships.

Here's my quick 2 cents on what organizations could be doing to keep internships alive:

1. Companies need to gain a better understanding of the law

2. Companies should put their staffs through training about how to manage an internship program

3. Companies should consider creating a letter of expectation that both the intern and the employer will sign

4. Colleges may have to step up to the plate and offer some incentives

5. Colleges could offer to subsidize the student pay for the company out of alumni contributions (and some have already done so)

6. Congress should offer incentives to companies, AS WELL as pay interns themselves!

Talk with your administrators to make sure they are aware of this ruling and the potential risks it presents for your students. You have an incredible opportunity to leverage this ruling to enlist the support and help of your management to adopt any of the above solutions.

NEW GRAD EMPLOYABILITY EXAM

10,000 hours of college experience will be
summed up in a 90 minute exam

 For decades employers have complained that graduates were not prepared for the transition from college to cubicle. Managers have moaned endlessly about how grads lacked the soft skills they need to become productive employees. This sentiment has been repeated in surveys, articles, blogs and meetings.

So who is responsible for preparing students for their first professional job?

* Employers think it's the responsibility of colleges.

* Colleges think it's the employer's responsibility.

* Students think it's the employer's responsibility.

No wonder we are at a stalemate and nothing is being done to solve this!

However, it's clear in these tight economic times that colleges can no longer ignore this situation. Because of this stalemate:

* Less grads will get hired.

* It will cost companies time and money to retrain grads to become productive employees.

It will affect your college enrollment too! Parents and prospective students will be looking for colleges that have high placement rates after college. If your placement rate is suffering, your enrollment revenue will drop.

So how are we going to solve this issue?

<u>Let's look first at why colleges are not accepting this responsibility.</u>

I don't have to remind you that your college curriculum is controlled by faculty. The curriculum and courses have been designed over the last two decades to ensure students have the knowledge required to be awarded their degree.

Your faculty are interested in their students mastering the data, skills and information relevant to their major, but not necessarily the skills they will need to succeed in their college to corporate transitions.

Faculty have little to no concern about what employers want or need. As a result, the curriculum focuses on what it takes to earn a degree in Asian art history, Ceramics, Journalism, French/German/Chinese, Music history, Bio chemistry, Hydrology, Nutrition or any of the hundreds of others available.

<u>Why do students expect businesses to train them?</u>

I was surprised to learn that students expect employers to train them.

Students graduate after investing up to 10,000 hours in study, class room activity, research, preparing reports, meeting in groups and extracurricular activity.

A poll by Accenture found that 77 percent of seniors expect their employer will provide training. Students believe they've done their part in investing the time and money to qualify for a degree.

However, the Accenture poll showed less than half, or 48%, of recent grads say they got training in their first year on the job.

Studies show it takes the average student nearly 8 months to get a job. Assuming your grads earn an average of $3,000 per month, they are losing $24,000 by not having the right skills employers are looking for.

<u>Why don't employers think this is their responsibility?</u>

A survey by Hart Research Associates found that 75% of employers polled wanted colleges to place more emphasis on critical thinking, complex problem-solving, written and oral communication and applied knowledge in real-world settings.

It also found that 93% of employers agreed that a candidate's ability to demonstrate the capacity to think critically, communicate clearly and solve complex problems was more important than his or her undergraduate major.

Over the past three decades, employers have repeatedly made their position clear to college administrators. Hiring managers generally do not care about the knowledge students have absorbed while in college as most of it is irrelevant to what they want them to do. Business leaders expect students to have the skills they need to hit the ground running and NOT have to retrain them.

But alas, few colleges agree.

Well, at least not for the moment!

You see a new test is being introduced that will give employers a way to select students, NOT by grade point, major and academic record, but by their ability to step into the firm and immediately provide a return on investment by solving production, operations, and/or revenue problems.

Grad Employability Exam

Employers have been looking for faster, better, cheaper, more efficient ways to hire your grads. The hiring process costs money and the HR department of employers, like yours are being forced to do a better job at hiring grads at less cost.

That means not only hiring the best talent that will immediately become an asset, but also talent that stays with the company.

A survey by Experience.com found that 70 percent of recent grads left their jobs within two years. Anything employers can do to increase the time new hires spend at the company will decrease the hiring cost and provide more experienced staff.

Hiring authorities have suggested there was no way to evaluate what students learned and/or if they were able to transfer that knowledge to be a productive worker. Without a formal test or way to evaluate their knowledge, companies end up hiring the wrong people that cost them a lot of time, and money to retrain.

What they have been looking for is a standardized test that will provide insight into how well a grad will fit in the company culture and measure their abilities.

The Collegiate Learning Assessment Plus is that test!

The Collegiate Learning Assessment Plus (CLA+) is being offered to graduating seniors at over 200 colleges in the Spring of 2014. Both small and state colleges are adopting the tests.

The test, developed by the Council for Aid to Education, a New York based nonprofit will cost grads $35 to take. Although the firm has contracts with colleges, the test is available to any grad, at any time, online.

The test will measure problem solving, writing, quantitative reasoning and reading and provide a number similar to SAT's that employers can use to rate and compare potential hires. Employers will very likely pay more attention to grads who test out with a perfect score of 1600 and will quickly overlook those below 1000. Grads will have only 90 minutes to complete the exam.

The test grew out of a similar exam that the Council for Aid to Education developed for college administrators to test students' knowledge at the start of their freshman year and then again at graduation. It helped colleges evaluate the effectiveness of their curriculum and gave them an opportunity to work with their faculty to make adjustments in order to improve students' scores.

This could be a paradigm shift:

- Grads with low GPA's could potentially do better and get hired

- Grads who do all the right things in taking ownership of their career might do poorly and get overlooked

These tests could have a significant impact on your graduates.

Companies and organizations may require students to take them and use the scores as a way of weeding out grads. If employers start requiring your students to take these courses, you'll have to adopt strategies to not only inform them about the test but also provide coaching on what to expect on the test and what they can do.

It's too early to determine how students will do!

But, it's a good time build a strategy and begin to prepare your students and grads for an exit exam that could significantly affect their employability.

WHY CAN'T JOHNNY FIND A JOB?

Graduates don't have a clue on how to find a job! That affects the reputation of your campus, degree, and diploma!

You've heard the phrase, "You can lead a horse to water, but you can't make it drink!"

I got thinking about this after talking to dozens of career professionals about students' lack of participation in the events and activities they provide. Story after story documented the time and effort they put into creating events to give students the knowledge and skills they needed to get jobs-- but alas, only a small number participated!

So why is that?

In talking to students and processing feedback from career professionals, there are many reasons why!

1. Students are busy completing their curriculum requirements, and don't have time or feel the pressure to build career and job search strategies

2. The career center is only open during class hours. It's inconvenient and doesn't fit in their schedules.

3. Students are not aware of the many services the career center can provide because the career center does not have the time to effectively market to them.

4. <u>The college has not put a priority on career education and job search strategies</u>. (We'll come back to this one!)

5. Students may have negative preconceived notions about the quality of services provided by the career center and assume they can pick up the skill sets on their own.

But can they?

Are graduates innate job hunters, born with the skills to master the job search gauntlet?

To find out, we organized a 12 hour GRAD Career Marathon where 24 career authors and coaches from around the world each shared 3 tips with grads. It was a massive effort! During the 12 hour career marathon we asked students,

"How much time each week do you spend looking for a job?"

We were curious because in a previous Webinar, Richard Bolles, author of *What Color Is your Parachute* shared that <u>studies indicated students spent about an hour a week looking for a job.</u> To us, that was a shocking number because it showed grads were simply not in the game. That could be a result of only two things:

• They didn't want to get a job

• They had no clue about how to look for a job

So, what was their response? <u>Over 60% of the students indicated they were spending 1-5 hours a week on their job searches!</u>

Wow. Richard Bolles was right! Now hold that thought...

That got me thinking about the stats career centers are being required to collect to show how many students are employed after graduation, how much they earned, etc.

What's behind this?

Recently, the American Bar Association agreed to provide graduate employment stats to US News & Report so they can include them as ranking stats. As a result, a college where grads are getting jobs will now be rated higher in the very popular college ranking list than a college where grads are not getting jobs.

In addition, congress passed legislation that initially requires for-profit colleges to collect and share employment stats with them and consumers! (Many suspect non-profit colleges will be required to do this in the future as well.)

Congress has two goals in mind. They want to make sure students:

• Can afford to pay back their loans and do not end up ruining their lives with misguided investments in their educations

• Are obtaining "Gainful Employment," or employment that is relevant to their degrees

Based on this new criteria, if your college ratings are below your competitors, and your students are struggling to pay back their student loans, your admissions departments will find it harder to recruit quality students, and your graduates will NOT be in a position to contribute to the annual giving and capital campaigns.

It's all related.

So where are we going with this blog post?

Well just in case I haven't made my point - YOUR grads don't have a clue about how to look for jobs. They don't understand the time and commitment required, and they don't have strategies! You need more proof? Remind your administrators that over the past 4 years 80 percent of grads nationwide were unemployed on the day they received their diplomas. 80 percent of those grads had to move home after graduation. Hardly a successful strategy!

Is this the career center's fault?

• No, you provided the opportunities and services to them.

• You've been there IF they needed you.

But, the bottom line, they didn't take advantage of your services! So forget about them! But you can't! If you do, you'll end up with poor stats that affect the revenue side of your college.

So what are you supposed to do?

The question is - not what you are supposed to do, but what your administration needs to do. Your administration needs to:

1. Require students to put in a MINIMUM amount of time and research into career development prior to graduation. We'd like to see this start their freshman years.

2. Integrate curriculum requirements with the end game in mind, helping students have successful careers.

3. <u>Provide you more resources instead of cutting them!</u>

4. And, create a culture on campus that involves faculty, athletics, staff and everyone that support the number one reason they are all there....

And that is to help graduates start successful careers - NOT get degrees based on certain curriculums. It only make sense:

1. Graduates get jobs quicker so they can pay back their loans and don't have to move back home

2. Admissions can pick from the best candidates

3. Annual giving and capital campaign treasure chests fill up!

It's a proactive strategy!

Unless your campus recognizes that and takes corrective action, you'll have the full weight of the government, the public, your students and alumni on your back! Trust me, that can be a pretty heavy experience. Just ask administrators of for-profit colleges!

Start a serious discussion with your management about this issue. Share with them articles about what the "firestorm" for profit career administrators faced when they were called to campus to testify. Encourage them to find a way to get ahead of this issue, before that happens.

WHEN WILL PARENTS AND STUDENTS REVOLT?

High cost of college, unemployment, loans,
credit card debt – ENOUGH!

Revolutions happen faster than anyone can predict!

During the uprising in Libya, the Obama administration was questioning why the CIA had not provided advance warning on what was boiling in Tunisia, Egypt, Jordan, Yemen, Sudan and other Middle Eastern countries.

I have to believe there were warning signs, and that the administration was informed, but nobody have could have predicted what event, what one thing, would drive a collective group of people to step out of their day to day struggle to survive to do like Howard Beal did in the movie, "Network" and scream, "I'm mad as hell and I'm not going to take it anymore!" (Search for it on YouTube, it's pretty neat to watch)

At any rate, that got me thinking about the situation parents and college students face today!

Consider some of these facts:

1. 80 percent of students move home after they graduate

2. Nearly 80%, or 2,774,008 of the 2009-2010 grads, were officially unemployed on graduation day.

3. 51% of student loan recipients say it will take them more than 10 years to pay off their student loans.

4. According to federal statistics, only 57% of full-time college students graduate within six years.

5. 1/3 of college grads hold jobs that do NOT require a college degree

Then ask yourself:

• Do you think parents and graduates are getting real returns on their investments?

• Do you think other businesses could survive if their product didn't do what they said it would do and it ended up costing customers more than they anticipated!

Who's got their head in the sand now?

Who is ignoring the facts and reports?

In Egypt anyone that had been close to Mubarak and his family were wise to run for cover as worldwide news organizations published via Social Media channels how a 30 year dictator and his colleagues had been stuffing their bank accounts and maintaining a lifestyle that supported homes around the world. Egyptians are gaining access to statistics and information long suppressed that are making them, "Mad as hell!"

On the other hand, the graduation and loan statistics I shared above have been readily available to college administrators, students and parents for some time. What surprises me is that students and parents seem to be resigned to the fact that they can't do anything about the issues they face.

College administrators seem to be focused on revenue and as long as they do not have to be accountable for these miserable stats, they seem comfortable ignoring them. <u>What if college students and their parents knew that the private colleges they were attending were spending $3,000 to recruit new students and only $85 to prepare them for their</u>

careers? (According to NACE the median budget for career centers is only $31,000. Also, State colleges spend approximately $1,000 to recruit a student.)

Shouldn't college students and their parents expect their colleges to do something to improve this situation?

In the 235 years since our nation was founded, we've been able to solve countless issues and seemingly impossible situations. Something can be done. But what?

Who is your elected officials listening to – Wall Street or YOU?

During the time our federal government bailed out Wall Street, banks and corporations around the country, our Congress, Senate and state legislatures have:

- Made sure that every college student that takes a student loan will NEVER be able to walk away from their debt.

- Passed legislation that has made it even more difficult for aspiring college students to get their own credit cards and credit.

- Passed legislation to continue to push the cost of education on to parents and students, even when evidence of the return on investment is dropping. (College tuition and fees increased 439 percent from 1982 to 2007 while median family income rose 147 percent.)

In the past 3 years, nearly 10 million graduates and parents have felt the effects of this legislation. But, still no uprising!

Tipping point!

So the question remains. When will students and parents reach their boiling point and say, "I'm mad as hell and I'm not going to take it anymore?"

Will it be when:

1. More students sue their alma mater like Trina Thomson did when she sued Monroe College for $72,000 (the full cost of her tuition)?

2. A significant number of students default on their loans?

3. Online education becomes a viable alternative and campus greens suddenly look like ghost towns?

4. Congress requires both for-profit and non-profit colleges to GUARANTEE their graduates "gainful employment"?

Your guess is as good as mine.

But something is boiling, and if your college want to be ahead of the game, they better be doing something to FIX these stats or their customers will consider their actions, too little, too late.

Just like citizens in Egypt did!

Help make a difference and bring about positive change. Ask your administrators to put themselves into the shoes of your students and their families and encourage them to listen to the stories of the unemployed, the underemployed alumni and ask them to support the ideas and strategies you are developing.

WHAT DOES YOUR COLLEGE OWE GRADUATES?

Jobs? Loan Repayment Guarantee? Training?

Over the past two years I've been watching what law schools are doing to offset the negative publicity they were getting from grads who were suing them for over-promising what they could expect to earn after they graduated.

Once identified as an ideal "professional" career and fueled by TV shows, from L.A. Law, Boston Legal, Law and Order, to the more recent Harry, the allure of earning a law degree has been tarnished by the news stories of the enormous additional cost, high number of industry layoffs, reduced hiring in the legal industry, and the frequent stories about grads suing their colleges. The real story is in the numbers. The industry has lost over 50,000 law-related jobs in the past five years but produces 40,000 new attorneys each year!

This constant bad press has resulted in a stunning fall in the number of people willing to pay between $75,000 to $125,000 for a law degree. As a result the number of applicants for law school has fallen from a peak of 100,000 in 2004 to an expected 54,000 in 2013. Less people are interested in joining an elite group of 1,200,000 working attorneys! That's probably good news for anyone that still wants to go to law school because there will be less competition for the seats available.

Law schools do the right thing!

I was surprised then to see that law schools did the right thing and decided to step up to the plate and offer more transparency to prospective students by showing data on the number of grads that had jobs within a period of time after graduation, and at what pay. Through their association, The American Bar Association, law schools agreed to provide U.S. News and World Report with this data and allow them to use it to rate a college. That means prospective students will be able to see which colleges produced the most grads, with the jobs after graduation, and what their annual salaries were.

Armed with that information prospective students will be able to make a decision about whether investing in a law degree from the college is worth it. (Interesting to note. Past surveys indicated lawyers earned an average of $4 million dollars in their lifetime)

In the past year, I've been hearing more government officials to talk about providing similar information to undergraduate students. While the data is still difficult for most colleges to collect, an online model has emerged to show prospective students and their parents how well grads are not only doing from a specific college, but by major too! President Obama considered this an important part of restructuring the student loan program and authorized the development of the College Scorecard.

As public funding for higher education is being cut by governors across the country, they ironically started to put more strings attached to the money they provided to encourage colleges to become more transparent to their prospective customers. In my State, Governor Kasich assembled a committee from the 43 public schools and challenges the design of a system that would reward them for the number of students that graduated. Other states are doing the same thing. Governors know their business leaders are looking for more educated workers and that voters with degrees will also pay more taxes.

Guaranteed job!

Now law schools are upping the game and creating law firms to absorb some of their grads each year. The Arizona State University Law School just announced the formation of a nonprofit organization they are calling the Alumni Law Group that will employ up to 30 graduates. The idea is to give more graduates an opportunity to hone their skills under the tutelage of professionals and give them a better chance of starting out their careers using the knowledge and skills they picked up in law school.

While the university is suggesting this program is being introduced to help give more people access to affordable attorneys, critics are suggesting this is just an attempt to fudge their numbers and rank higher on the U.S. News and World Report. Being able to report 30 more grads having a job each year immediately after graduation could be worth the time and investment in a program like this.

So that brings me to the point of this blog article...

What does your college owe your graduates?

Do you think you owe them a job for investing the cost of an average American home for their education?

Loan Repayment

A number of colleges are experimenting with the idea of guaranteeing students that after they graduate, if they are not earning enough to pay back their loans, the college will step in to help. Alma College, Tufts University, Spring Arbor University and Huntington University are among them. Colleges are paying the LRAP Association roughly $1,200 per student year to provide a fund that will guarantee the loan repayment. While it does increase the cost of education, it provides a safe landing spot for students after they graduate.

Additional Training

Gwinnett Technical College says, "If one of our graduates who was educated under a standard program and his/her employer agrees that the employee is deficient in one or more competencies as defined in the standards, the technical college will retrain that employee at no instructional cost to employee or employer."

The key here is that your college recognizes that it's no longer business as usual. For unusual times, unusual strategies and plans are necessary. It doesn't matter to me what you do, only that you get management to start thinking out of the box to providing solutions all grads and alumni.

Students put their faith in your college when they elected to pay their tuition and direct state funding to your campus. Now is the time to show them that their faith was not misguided.

"What we find changes who we become."

— <u>Peter Morville</u>

7

RESEARCH TO BUILD YOUR STRATEGIES ON

GRAD/ALUMNI SATISFACTION

OPINIONS OF HIRING MANAGERS AND CAREER PROFESSIONALS

You don't need to do much research to know something is broken in the way we prepare students for their first professional job search. You are living with the issues, the shortcomings and the problems created by decades old administrative policies of a campus culture that does not focus on careers and an ever declining budget preventing you from implementing changes.

If you are going to build a strong case on why you need to go forward with your vision and plan, management will need stats, facts and research they can share their advisors and the board of trustees.

So this chapter takes a look at some of the more relevant studies that offer strong evidence that something, anything needs to be done right now to change a situation that is failing in many cases the MAJORITY of graduates.

To get the attention of your management, write a brief summary of the issues your campus if facing and put a big, jinormous, fat F on the front of the report to draw attention to how you feel the college is doing in supporting the career needs of students, grads and alumni.

The fifth report we look at is, A Roadmap for Transforming the College-To-Career Experience. It's a crowd sourced whitepaper compiled and edited by Andy Chan and Tommy Derry and provides dozens of new strategies and best practices of career professionals like you who are introducing positive, relevant change with an eye of creating a career centered College Culture! I strongly urge you to pick it up and offer the examples of what peer institutions management are supporting. Many times all it takes is to let management know they are running the risk of falling behind competitors.

You can turn the tide and change the culture with this research.

Here are the 5 topics we'll discuss:

1. Survey of 635 Career Professionals Suggest Grads' Resumes ARE NOT Job Search Ready!

2. Employers Are Not Thrilled With The Quality of Your Grads - Is Your President Listening?

3. Graduates Lack "Soft Skills" Needed in the College to Corporate Transition

4. McKinsey and Company Report Confirms - Grads Not Ready for the Marketplace

5. Best practices and examples of organizations who are RETHINKING SUCCESS.

SURVEY OF CAREER PROFESSIONALS SUGGEST GRADS' RESUMES ARE NOT JOB SEARCH READY!

This report screams that the current career services model is broken and your management need to read this!

A new study by the Career Advisory Board that was conducted by the National Association of Colleges and Employers (NACE) finds career center professionals regard graduates as "academically prepared, but not marketplace ready."

Of the college career center directors surveyed, 56% cite students' lack of interest in formal career preparation and professional development as barriers to successfully finding jobs.

The survey found that career center professionals believe the biggest obstacle for students in finding jobs after graduation is their unrealistic expectations of the amount of effort and motivation it takes to get jobs. Previous surveys by NACE show students simply don't use the career center. In their Benchmark 2011 report, a survey of seniors showed that over 60% either NEVER went to the career center, or visited less than twice!

Could this have some impact on why, according to the Associated Press, approximately 1.5 million, or 53.6 percent, of bachelor's degree-holders under the age of 25 are jobless or underemployed in the United States?

We think so!

A survey TalentMarks did of graduates found that 95% did not have a written job search strategy and 60% of grads spent 5 or less hours a week on their job searches. In our discussions with graduates the principal reason they did not spend more time on their job searches is that they exhausted their options and didn't know what else to do! With limited job search knowledge, the typical grad will post a bunch of resumes on job boards, sigh and then resign themselves to the fact that they did everything they could to get a job that day!

The survey was conducted by the National Association of Colleges and Employers (for CAB) suggests grads are CLUELESS about how to get a job!

Check out these numbers shared by four year colleges!

When asked if students have their resumes ready to start professional job searches:

- 9.4 percent strongly disagreed

- 43.3 percent disagreed

- 19.3 percent neither agreed or disagreed

- 25 percent agreed

- 2.8 percent strongly agreed

And the response from two year colleges was worse!

- 39.0 percent strongly disagreed

- 44.1 percent disagreed

- 8.5 percent neither agreed or disagreed

- 8.5 percent agree

- NOBODY strongly agreed!

Does this surprise you?

It did me, as resume development is the number one primary service many career centers provide.

I didn't interpret these numbers to suggest the career center is doing a horrible job in teaching students how to develop professional resumes, but as the result of a very small number of students who visit the career center. Don't believe me? In a previous blog article, we shared that a NACE 2011 survey showed over 60 percent of graduating seniors either NEVER went to the career center or visited only 1 or 2 times.

That's barely enough time to develop a professional resume!

So what can we do?

One of the solutions we've been working on for the past two years is an online resume course taught by the New York Times bestselling author Martin Yate. Martin helped us create a 3 session course that will give students a foundation in understanding the fundamentals of creating a resume and how to make resumes work for them.

For career centers, it's an incredible tool.

Instead of having to repeat the same information to 500 students over and over, students are encouraged to take Martin's course, do the assignments and then go to the career center where career counselors can spend more time helping the student polish their resume and take them to the next level. And because the course is available anytime, through any device, students can "fit" it into their busy schedules.

Nearly every department on your campus is frantically looking at ways to adopt online learning strategies to not only be relevant to the changing behaviors of students as well as the incredible new technologies that are shaping the change, but department leaders and your President are trying to remain competitive.

You can remind management of the need to build an eLearning platform to deliver online career curriculum at anytime, anyplace through any device.

EMPLOYERS ARE NOT THRILLED WITH THE QUALITY OF YOUR GRADS - IS YOUR PRESIDENT LISTENING?

Your campus could place more grads by listening and acting on the needs of the companies that hire your grads.

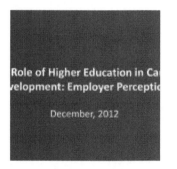

Prediction - In the future companies will rate colleges on how well they prepare grads for their first professional jobs. Colleges that rate poorly will see a slump in enrollment, and their grads will have a harder time getting hired at the best organizations.

Over the past 5 years, there have been a number of reports issued that showed students wished they had done more to prepare for their first professional jobs and even more reports that showed hiring authorities complaining that the grads they were hiring were not ready for the workplace.

Now, yet another study suggests employers are having trouble finding recent graduates that are qualified to fill positions at their companies or organizations. The survey by The Chronicle and American Public Media's Marketplace found that:

- An astonishing 53% either answered they had a difficult, or very difficult time filling their positions with recent grads.

- Nearly 33% gave colleges fair to poor marks for producing successful grads.

- 28% of hiring authorities and business leaders felt the value of a bachelor's degree had diminished.

Your president can either ignore this information, or see it as an incredible opportunity to reach out to hiring authorities to see how your college and career center can make it easier for companies to hire the right people, gain an understanding about why hiring authorities thought colleges were producing less than successful graduates, and more importantly, shore up the reputation and VALUE of the diploma they award successful graduates!

In this survey, employers acknowledge as other studies have, that grads were well versed in the knowledge required by their professors to earn their degrees, but they lacked basic workplace proficiencies, including adaptability, communication skills, leadership and the creative ability to solve complex problems.

It seems a bachelor's degree is an important sorting tool for hiring managers but it's clear from this and other studies that graduates are falling short of their expectations.

Hiring authorities look to your college as a supplier and will hold YOU accountable!

This is not a new issue. Businesses have been sharing this frustration for decades. College presidents need to be worried that business leaders sooner or later will take matters into their own hands and try to solve this problem on their own.

In fact it's already happening.

In 2008, The Boeing Company created a system to rank colleges on how well their graduates performed within their company. Imagine that! <u>Boeing was holding colleges responsible, just like they hold their suppliers responsible to deliver product to them.</u>

To Boeing, there was no debate about who is responsible to get grads up to speed for their first professional jobs. Their message to college administrators is,

"If you want your grads to have a shot at working at Boeing, you will have to deliver the kind of grad we want!"

Right now, the political and economic climate is pushing colleges to capture:

- The earnings of grads/alumni.

- How quickly after graduation grads get jobs.

- If the job grads get are relevant to their degrees.

Now, here is a company that developed a formula to evaluate how quickly graduates were able to transition to the business world and provide creative, timely and relevant solutions to the issues their company was facing!

Boeing kept this information confidential and shared it with colleges that were interested. As you might suspect, colleges that paid attention, listened, and adjusted their curriculums to accommodate Boeing's thoughtful research and conclusions are seeing more of their grads getting hired at Boeing. For colleges that could not change their cultures and get their faculties to adapt their curriculums, or simply ignored Boeing's requests--those grads have to work extremely hard to even get their resumes looked at.

Businesses don't like to make mistakes. In their world, they don't have time for oversights --so more and more of them will learn to work with the limited number of colleges that listen to them. General Electric is doing just that. The company concentrates its recruitment on just 45 US and 60 foreign campuses, from which it makes 2/3rds of its hires. Any college administration that ignores this trend is missing out on a guaranteed pipeline that can place their graduates and give their students internships.

Whose responsibility it is to prepare grads doesn't need to be debated!

As more companies adopt this technique, smart college presidents will read the tea leaves and understand that this represents an opportunity for them to not only increase enrollment, at a higher price, but to also help alumni be more successful. Successful presidents will engage faculties and staffs to take leadership positions in these areas.

However, it's not going to be easy!

Most faculties I talk to characterize this as an unsolvable problem. In fact, I saw a recent quote by a faculty member who tried to make light of the situation by saying, "I understand that those doing the hiring in ancient Greece complained about the same thing."

They don't see this as their responsibilities to listen to what hiring authorities say their managers want. Most fervently believe their jobs are to cram students heads full of the curriculum required to get a degree, but unless students are STEM students, it's unlikely the knowledge they picked up to qualify for their degrees and majors are going to support the day to day needs of employers.

So is it an employer's responsibility to bring grads up to speed for that first professional job search? Businesses don't think so.

And neither does the University of Phoenix!

In a previous chapter I shared a new strategy that University of Phoenix adopted which resulted in an army of staff reaching out to business leaders to find out what they wanted. That's right, University of Phoenix has over 2,000 staff who have been reaching out to business leaders to find out what kinds of skills and knowledge they want in their graduates.

They ask questions, and then they listen!

- What skills and knowledge do new hires not have that you want?

- What kind of curriculum should we provide our students that would benefit you?

- What traits, behaviors and attitudes are you looking for?

Is your college reaching out to hiring authorities and asking these questions?

So I have to ask you: Who is your college's client?

The University of Phoenix believes the companies that hire their grads are their clients.

Why do they think this?

Michael Mayor, Senior Vice President of Education to Careers at the University of Phoenix acknowledges that the student is paying Phoenix for the degree, and to most people would consider the student the customer, but, their research confirms the reason their students are going to <u>college is to get great jobs, and launch career paths that will help them achieve their dreams</u>.

To do that, they need to get hired.

Michael acknowledges management was in agreement with this philosophy, and was willing to give him VAST amounts of funding to field a team that could go out and "listen" to hiring authorities' needs. More importantly, management bought into the concept at the highest levels and reinforced the idea throughout all areas of the company, particularly with the faculty and curriculum designers. That enabled the college to, over time, revamp their courses and curriculum to make them more relevant to EMPLOYERS' needs, rather than keep up with academic trends within the industry.

Trust me, this trend is not going to go away.

Business leaders will begin to EXPECT colleges to listen to them. Their professional trade groups, conferences and news channels will spread this idea rapidly. In fact, another report just issued by Accenture--their 2013 College Graduate Employment Survey-- suggests that companies work closely with educational institutions to engage in curriculum development and create customized training and industry credential programs.

In order to position your college as a leader, you will need to get the president and his/her team on board. They will help you lead the charge to approach faculty and curriculum designers to build a curriculum around supporting the needs of companies that hire your grads.

What's at stake?

I'm convinced organizations that fail to listen to the needs of employers will find their enrollments drop because of the trend in reporting hiring trends of grads, and their grads and alumni will find it harder to get the kind of jobs they deserve.

Businesses are already lining up to do business with colleges that are paying attention to them. Sit down with your management to discuss which employers you'd like to see hire more of your grads and invite them to campus to meet a small group including upper management and faculty. Your goal will be to get faculty and upper management to hear what you already know.

Many times it sounds different coming from an authority they "have" to listen to.

GRADUATES LACK "SOFT SKILLS" NEEDED IN THE COLLEGE TO CORPORATE TRANSITION

Place more grads in jobs by providing them the
soft skills business leaders are looking for

We've been doing a great deal of research lately concerning how to help graduates manage the campus to corporate transition.

A great deal is at stake.

Companies spend an enormous amount of money in finding and acquiring the right talent, yet are confronted with students who lack the basic understanding of the how to work within a team environment, that are driven by work ethics that support the companies missions, exhibits basic communication and writing skills, and know how to support and work for a boss.

As a result, although the candidates might have been the brightest in their classes, they quite possibly lack, "people skills", motivation or commitments to any of the characteristics mentioned above.

This is a problem that is not just found in the US. In an article I ran across today in the Guardian of the UK, the author identified similar issues businesses and grads are facing:

The report Chartered Institute of Personnel and Development (CIPD), the TUC and think tank, the Institute for Public Policy Research, says: "Compared to other northern European countries, young people in the UK are largely left to navigate the transition to work and responsible adulthood alone, and the support they receive varies wildly across different families, communities and employers."

In another article in the Birmingham News by Roy Williams, another survey outlines why graduates are likely to be unemployed for some time to come:

Lack of jobs, not qualifications, is the top reason recent college graduates and post-graduates are unemployed and likely to remain so, according to "The Hiring of 2012 University/ College Undergraduates and Postgraduates" survey by the Society of Human Resource Management, a national trade group that has an active chapter in Birmingham.

"What do graduates today bring to the job? They're likely to be savvy in technology," said Mark Schmit, the organization's vice president of research in a release. "Still, they must improve basic skills/knowledge, such as English grammar and spelling, and applied skills, such as critical thinking, to best compete for jobs and transition into the ones they land."

To solve this problem, we are in the process of developing a comprehensive solution that will:

- Provide an online soft skills curriculum to college students

- Deliver the services through any device, at any time

- Utilize social media to increase participation

- Recognize and reward participating students with Badges and social media recognition

This program is designed to help students quickly navigate the campus to corporate transition in a fun, scalable and measurable way. Students/ Grads with these skills will be hired more as companies feel more confident they will gain employees that will start out being productive and help to cut costs and produce revenue.

John Norris, an economist and managing director of wealth management at Birmingham's Oakworth Capital Bank confirms this,

"Given the overall sluggishness of business conditions, businesses are looking for candidates who can come in and make a relatively immediate impact on the bottom line. Each business will have its own timeline for new employees, but I imagine very few are looking to make an investment in an employee who may or may not pan out in three to five years."

If your college is interested in helping more students get jobs and immediately become productive employees, contact me. We've got some ideas we've been discussing with other colleges that are designed to deliver the kind of soft skills your students need.

Your focus on improving their soft skills will increase retention, cut recruitment costs, and help a generation become more successful in building successful careers!

MCKINSEY AND COMPANY REPORT CONFIRMS - GRADS NOT READY FOR THE MARKETPLACE

Significant research of 8,000 executives provide direction your management can take

Voice of the graduate

Now another study by McKinsey, in collaboration with Chegg, surveyed nearly 5,000 college graduates to gauge their attitudes on a range of issues.

Their report is called *Voice of the Graduate*.

I've been impressed with McKinsey's focus on education. A previous and exhaustive report, *Education to Employment*, surveyed 8,000 executives and examined 100+ best education best practices. McKinsey is looking at the long political, economic and human costs of a generation of workers who are unemployed or underemployed. Their reports are attempting to get business leaders and higher education professionals to the same table to discuss how they can help more grads transition with the RIGHT knowledge and skills to their first professional jobs.

The results of *Voice of the Graduate* to a large extent were predictable. The study showed:

1. Students felt unprepared for the world of work.

2. Half of those surveyed indicated they would have picked another major or different school if they had to do it all over again.

3. A large percent didn't do due diligence in their college searches to explore stats and facts about college graduation and employment rates.

4. Most graduates adopt a "do it yourself" approach to their job searches.

5. The VAST majority of grads do NOT use their college career center or tap into their alumni networks.

The report suggests these graduates are entering a world where their knowledge and skills are mismatched for the jobs available in the workplace. The types of jobs in demand today are different than those 20 years ago. Jobs today require specialized skills that graduates are not acquiring through their college courses. Business leaders are sharing their concerns about this issue and looking to colleges for solutions.

The report identified 8 key findings from the research on student attitudes and poised questions we ask ourselves on how we can improve or fix the situation that is affecting grads. The 8 key findings are that grads:

1. are overqualified

2. are under prepared

3. have regrets

4. haven't done homework

5. are disappointed

6. are asking "Can I help you?"

7. are suffering the choice of Liberal arts

8. are taking a do-it-yourself attitude

8 Key Findings:

Grads Are Over Qualified

Students in the study echoed student sentiments from a recent analysis from the US Bureau of Labor Statistics which showed that 48 percent of employed US college graduates are in jobs that require less than a four year college education. The most important question they asked in this area was:

> *Are there ways to better tailor the educational experience to employer needs and student prospects, both as a matter of skill acquisition and cost effectiveness?*

Grads Are Under prepared

According to the survey, one-third of graduates of four-year colleges did not feel college prepared them well for employment. The authors suggested we think out of the box.

> *Is it a paradox that so many graduates feel overqualified, yet also under prepared – or does it suggest that colleges could offer more courses and programs aimed directly at "life skills" needed for success in the workplace?*

Grads Have Regrets

The survey found that if they had to do it all over again, 53 percent of grads would have done something differently, for example--chosen a different major, or gone to a different college. To start a discussion on your campus the authors suggested you ask the following question:

> *Although some desire for "do-overs" may be inevitable, would greater efforts to educate high-school students about how to judge their potential fit with institutions and fields help reduce regrets? Are there examples of success in this area that could be studied and expanded?*

Grads Haven't Done Their Homework

Policy makers, including the president, governors and the media are forcing colleges to help educate parents and students about how effective their educations have been to help grads get jobs and build successful careers.

The study showed half of graduates did not look at graduation rates when picking a college, and four in ten didn't look at job placement or salary records. The authors suggested we ask ourselves:

> *Should colleges and universities take bolder steps to track and publish such data voluntarily in order to stem the drive for new laws and regulations that may place unreasonable burdens on them and create unintended consequences?*

Grads Are Disappointed

The survey found that half of the nation's graduates could not find work in the fields they had hoped for. Graduating from the country's top schools didn't help much in this area. Four of ten grads from the top 100 colleges couldn't get jobs in their chosen fields! Two important questions the authors suggest you ask on your campus are:

> *Are there better ways to educate high-school students about potential opportunities in different fields so that they develop more realistic expectations about their chances for employment?*
>
> *Does the scale of unmet expectations suggest that colleges need to improve their career counseling functions, and how?*

Grads Are Asking "Can I help you?"

The annual UCLA HERI survey of incoming freshman showed that 88 percent are going to college to improve their chances of getting good jobs. However, this study found that 6 times as many graduates are working in retail or hospitality as those who originally noted a desire to work in those fields. This year 120,000 graduates will "settle" for jobs as waiters, salespeople, cashiers and baristas. The authors ask:

> *If retail and restaurant jobs are destined to be fast-growing categories of work, are there ways to rethink the value proposition of these jobs so that more graduates feel happier choosing them?*

Grads Are Suffering the Choice of Liberal Arts

Graduates who majored in liberal arts and performing arts fare the worst across every measure; they tend to be lower paid, deeper in debt, less happily employed and slightly more likely to wish they'd done things differently. <u>Knowing this, why couldn't the deans of the colleges take a more active role in helping their students understand how to</u>

communicate to prospective employers about how their knowledge and skills prepare them to manage the jobs at hand? A question to consider asking your deans is:

> *How might educational institutions and stakeholders galvanize new efforts so that the many benefits of a liberal-arts education do not come at the expense of employment prospects?*

Grads Choose a Do-it-Yourself Attitude

This one hurts anyone involved in career education. According to the study, less than 40 percent of graduates used career services and less than **30 percent tapped into alumni networks to find jobs.** Ouch! A rare insight was offered by students on what the career center could have done that would have encouraged them to use those resources:

- 23 percent across all institution types would have liked a career placement service.

- 18 percent would have liked an opportunity for real world experience.

- 13 percent would have liked more practical skills development in class.

An important question rarely asked in attempting to better prepare students for the college-to-corporate transition was:

> *What role might life-skills programs play in improving the transition from college to employment?*

How can you get more students to take ownership of their careers?

Engage parents and encourage them to encourage their son or daughter to take ownership of their careers the minute they set foot on campus. I mentioned it before, but this would be another appropriate time to remind you to check out the CareerParents Online Community TalentMarks created to engage parents and encourage students to utilize the services of the career center.

Summary

The McKinsey/Chegg report, *The Voice of the Graduate*, was not designed to offer solutions but to give a voice to the millions of graduates entering the workplace who will be shocked to learn their $100,000 investment did not position them for jobs within their fields or even their interests.

You don't have to spend a dime to learn what you need to do. The report offered the following suggestions:

- Provide more experiential learning opportunities, from internships and co-op work to meaningful volunteer opportunities.

- Provide modules about workplace skills that give students an essential grounding in how to function effectively in professional environments.

- Provide more transparency concerning the return on investment a student will get from his or her education by providing graduation rates, times to employment, and salary ranges. More importantly, train families and students to use the information constructively.

My hope is this report will give politicians, parents, administrators and prospective students a better understanding of the issues graduates are facing and that each will use the information to enact change.

CAREER CENTER PROFESSIONALS ARE – RETHINKING SUCCESS

Industry insiders' pool strategies to create a
career centered college culture

In the foreword to this book, Robert Shindell suggested that the current career services model was broken. It is broken because it is failing a LARGE number of the people whom was designed to serve and the organizations that hire them.

Robert was not pointing a finger at career professionals who are stuck with the tasks of trying to provide relevant services to students and alumni in an era of declining budgets. He is not placing blame on administrators who are daily faced with trying to motivate students to take ownership of their careers, with an administrations who look the other way when presented facts, stats and public opinions that suggest they are not doing enough to help students launch their careers.

No, Robert is suggesting that the processes, methodologies and systems developed during the "Leave it to Beaver Era" are just not working in an era where a tight job market is making the process of getting a job as competitive as the playoffs during March Madness. Getting a job today requires an aggressive sophistication and an understanding of the entire ecosystem that encompasses job search knowledge and skills.

An ongoing stream of surveys of hiring authorizes, grads, and career professionals confirms that no one is happy with the way things are, but few in leadership positions are stepping forward to give career professionals the freedom and resources they need to craft a more relevant career services model.

That may be changing however!

A trail blazing report issued by industry professionals is showing that a trend is starting to bring about transformational career service changes at campuses where leadership "gets it"!

It all started...

In April 2012 more than 250 higher education administrators, faculty members, corporate executives, and national thought leaders met at Wake Forest University to discuss and evaluate the role and value of a liberal arts education in the 21st century work force.

The attendees represented career professionals and college administrators that were not happy with "business as usual" practices and knew there was mounting evidence that the system was failing. They gathered to share problems, discuss issues and look for inspiration to bring about transformative change to their colleges.

The organizers of the meeting invited career professionals to bring their stats, facts and creativity, and participate in a lively discussion designed to inspire and encourage action.

The goal of the 3 day events was to:

1. Collect benchmark best practices and ideas.
2. Gather ideas, data, trends and perspectives from others outside of higher education.
3. Connect like-minded thinkers.
4. Reflect strategically on current office practices, methodologies, and the roles they play in their organizations.
5. Be able to accurately articulate of the value of a liberal arts education.
6. Build excitement about the road ahead!

Michael Selverian, the former Managing Director of Gamma Capital Ltd., helped lift spirits and offer career professionals proof that the climate is right for them to be suggesting transformational change. According to Michael,

"University and college presidents, administrators and career development officers are keenly aware that the price and value of a liberal arts education is being questioned. Rather than reacting defensively, they are deeply examining their programs and defining key objectives to frame personal and career development as an imperative component of higher education's mission."

He encouraged attendees to take advantage of this trend and get involved in the discussion on their campuses.

Dr. Phil Gardner, the Director of Research for the Collegiate Employment Research Institute, shared with the group facts to help them understand how the problem needs to be addressed from the prospective of the employer. Dr. Gardner's research suggested liberal arts colleges:

- Help their students understand how to articulate and demonstrate their abilities in order to perform well in the job search and interview processes.

- Students should be taught several key technical and professional skills that are highly valued – and often required – by employers.

The three-day event created new friendships, a sense of mutual understanding, and a desire to keep the conversation going. To accomplish all of this, participants were encouraged to share ideas and any changes they were making on their own campuses.

Andy Chan, Vice President for Personal and Career Development, and Thomas Derry, Wake Forest Fellow in the Office of Personal and Career Development, collected the ideas and responses of participants and produced a crowd sourced paper, *A Roadmap for Transforming the College-To-Career Experience*. It's worth a read and can be quickly found by doing an internet search. However, if you don't have the time, let me give you a quick summary.

The report identifies three primary ideas and themes attendees were taking back to their campuses that would help them build strategies to address:

- Institutional leadership

- Career Office Vision and Innovation

- Higher Education Value Proposition

As we have repeatedly stated in this book, the attendees collectively agreed that the only way a campus can make transformative change and move in the direction of a career centered college culture is to get leadership engaged, involved and supportive. The report suggests:

> A top insight reported by a number of attendees is that institutional leadership and support is absolutely essential in order to create an environment where personal and career development is mission critical.

Attendees felt that it would be necessary for them to be involved in evaluating, adapting and/or outright changing the vision, mission and goals of the campus. The report suggests that colleges look to make a dramatic break from the past in order to bring about authentic transformation. Ron Albertson, director of the Career Office at Reed College suggested that resources cannot dictate vision. The report goes on to say:

> If vision is limited by the current set of circumstances, transformative change will not occur. A vision that inspires, that addresses a challenge, and that unites constituents will find backing, both financial and otherwise.

What are the common themes you hear about college today?

The attendees decided that the third most important takeaway they had was to try to find a way to frame the burning question heard at the water cooler, at the corner drug store, and across every media channel, "What is the value of a college education today?" Instead of sticking their heads in the sand and ignoring this question as so many in leadership positions continue to do, this group vowed to start an open, authentic discussion and use that discussion to formulate policy change.

Ideas implemented from attendees

If you are like me, you've been to countless conferences and came home with buzz of excitement and armed with dozens of ideas you want to implement, but--as they say--life gets in the way and as the days turn to weeks, and the weeks to months, you find the ideas slipping away and become a mere dream. That's not what happened for this charged-up group.

According to the report a number of participants went back to their colleges and starting kicking up dust!

- Tom Brinkley the Executive Director for the Student Professional Development Center of Elon University decided to focus on their first generation students and build a support process to ensure student success as well as create a reward system called the College 2 Career Student Rewards Program to encourage students to take ownership of their careers.

- Chris Howard, the President of Hampden-Sydney College and Rucker Snead, the newly titled Associate Dean for Career Education and Vocational Reflection, introduced a new program called Tiger Tracks which assists students in navigating the path from college into different industries.

- Hope College decided to fully utilize the Clifton Strengths Finder Assessment by working with the residence hall staff to encourage more students to take assessments. To further support the importance and commitment of the college, they reached out and got the support of faculty advisors to incorporate assessment tools in their first year seminar courses.

- At Messiah College, Dr. Peter Powers is challenging his colleagues to find ways they can help students better articulate the connection between what they are learning in their disciplines and the world of work.

- Michigan State University has developed "Neighborhoods" where MSU resources are brought to students where they live. Career information discussions occurring along with discussions related to campus life, and health, and even academic classes offered where they are are making the career center less of a destination.

- Meredith Maw, the Assistant Vice President and Executive Director of the Career Advancement Office at the University of Chicago, introduced a new program to offer very personal coaching and advising to students. Students with similar interests were brought together and over a 5-week period and were given concentrated career building guidance.

- President Nathan Hatch envisioned Wake Forest University as a campus whose culture is infused with personal and career development. His vision saw students not only acquiring an academic education, but a career education too! To implement the strategy he appointed Andy Chan to a cabinet position as the Vice President for Personal and Career Development. Instead of slashing the career center budget, President Hatch raised 10 million dollars to build a state-of-the-art office for the career center as well as all the necessary, relevant resources it might need and staffing to run it.

- Noah Levitt, the Assistant Dean for Student Engagement at Whitman College also reached out to faculty to integrate career education within the current curriculum. Noah also implemented a Fellows program, modeled after one introduced by Wake Forest, which gives recent graduates an opportunity to work for different administrative offices as part of their roles in academic projects.

So how do you start – RETHINKIING SUCCESS on your campus?

Andy Chan compiled the feedback from attendees and identified 7 key steps you should take to not only develop a vision for where you want to take your career center but to put your department at the center of your student's activities.

It's just like baking a cake! Follow these steps to develop a career centered college culture:

1. Develop a bold vision and mission for personal and career development.

2. Secure backing from institutional leadership.

3. Strategically position the personal and career development leadership role.

4. Strategically transform, build, and align personal and career development organization and staff.

5. Gather and report personal and career development outcome data to all constituents.

6. Engage and equip a college-to-career community of influencers, with a focus on faculty and parents.

7. Implement programs so personal and career development is a mission critical component of a student's college experience.

So there you have it—

It's a perfect recipe to create a career centered college culture!

Don't forget to give a shout out to the team that is taking the first step to help transform the industry!

Then to get started, I would advise you to write a-one page report identifying why your campus needs to be moving towards a career centered college culture and clip a copy of *Rethinking Success, A Roadmap for Transforming the College-to-Career Experience* and attach to it. Next, ask for a time to meet to discuss the issues. At that meeting, stress the fact that other institutions are marching down this path already and remind those in the meeting that you assume they don't want to be the people responsible for letting your college fall behind its competitors.

Good luck!

"The man who graduates today and stops learning tomorrow is uneducated the day after."

~Newton D. Baker

8 REACH ALUMNI WITH SCALABLE CAREER SERVICES

The research we shared in an earlier chapter by Olsen Zaltman Associates clearly showed that alumni are looking for career oriented programming and services. According to the research, alumni look to their alma mater as a trusted source to help them through the transitions in their lives.

While the traditional "Leave it to Beaver" role for alumni relations is to engage alumni in events and activities to strengthen their loyalty and imbue a sense of responsibility to support annual giving and capital campaigns, the new approach is more about providing "value added" services that extend their learning and knowledge in the phases they go through from getting their first job, buying a house, starting a family, career changes, health issues and ultimately retirement.

The new focus for alumni relations is to continue to support alumni to ensure they have a successful life, no matter how they define that.

This collection of mini-chapters will examine this trend and help you see what role your department could play in better serving alumni. By changing the way you serve alumni you open more opportunities to gain their expertise and commitment to students and campus needs.

Let's review strategies that are inclusive of alumni!

Here are the 4 topics we'll discuss:

1. Your Alumni Want You to Provide Career Coaching & Job Placement Services!

2. The Jury Is In! Your Alumni Want Help Networking!

3. 3 Ways to Help Alumni Get Jobs

4. Annual Mentoring Campaign!

YOUR ALUMNI WANT YOU TO PROVIDE CAREER COACHING & JOB PLACEMENT SERVICES!

This is the number two request of alumni from a survey of alumni

In a previous chapter, I outlined how your college could use LinkedIn and Facebook to help alumni expand their professional networks. Coming in a close second and third were requests for career coaching and job placement. <u>Both topics were, by a large margin, more requested than resume help.</u> This floored us!

Why?

I spent over a decade building alumni online communities and interacting with alumni professionals. I've attended nearly 100 CASE conferences around the US, Europe and Asia, and to the best of my ability, I can't recall engaging in a conversation or witnessing a presentation that suggested that the alumni association or career center provide career coaching and job placement services to alumni!

But, as Bob Dylan said over 4 decades ago, "The times they are a changing."

•   Since the economy crashed in 2008, the unemployment rate for workers with college degrees has doubled.

- The average grad today will take nearly 8 months to find a job.

- According to a survey the Associated Press, 53.6 percent of grads 25 and younger are either unemployed or under employed.

With these and a multitude of other changes happening in the employment market, doesn't it make sense to add in or modify some events and activities to focus on career and professional development programming?

The rise of organizations like the Alumni Career Services Network as well as the increased discussions on the topic by alumni boards and alumni staffs are likely to result in more alumni associations and career centers adding goal statements designed to implement strategies that will help alumni build successful careers.

Who should provide career coaching?

Is this the responsibility of the alumni association or the career center? With the average career center still reeling from an 8 percent budget cut over the last couple of years, it would be unrealistic to expect career center staffs to have the time to design marketing programs and then make time for the rush of alumni who are expected to take advantage of the programs.

On the other hand, while alumni professionals are brilliant at building relationships and engaging alumni, most would admit they do not have the academic or professional backgrounds to offer career coaching to alumni --*Not to mention the lack of time!*

So how can your college deliver on the second most requested career service of alumni? It's Simple:

By using the talents and passion of alumni who are career coaches.

It doesn't matter if you have 10,000 or 600,000 alumni, within your alumni base there are hundreds, if not thousands, of alumni who are independent coaches with the skills sets and passions to help people develop successful career strategies. All you need to do is develop a program that brings their talents to the attention of your alumni.

What about a job placement service?

This is a bit trickier.

In the traditional sense, job placement involves someone actively marketing a client and working on his/her behalf to find a job for that individual.

However, there are a couple of ways your alumni association can still help alumni in this area.

First, consider adding a job board to your alumni career site.

Again, it doesn't matter if you have 10,000 or 600,000 alumni, you have alumni that work for thousands of companies -- all of which will hire from time to time. I'd suggest you encourage alumni to share your job board with the hiring authorities in their firms. It's a known fact that 80 percent of the jobs that are offered come from within one's network. Implementing a program like this could not only give your alumni an inside track on jobs, but alert them to jobs before they are even posted! We are introducing to our CareerWebinars for Alumni clients a free job board that works like eHarmony. It will match alumni to jobs already posted at thousands of job boards around the country as well as alert them when new jobs are posted that match their skills and experience. The program will also generate revenue for the alumni association from job postings.

Second, hold a Talent-a-thon in the spring!

Another way to help alumni get jobs is to marshal your alumni support for those that don't have jobs through a Spring Talent-a-thon.

In a previous chapter, I shared how you could use the talents of your annual giving phone crew to call alumni and ask them to mentor incoming freshmen in the fall, as well as support the hiring of fellow alumni. The fundraising industry likes to remind us that alumni have Time, Treasures and Talents to give. In this case, the Talent-a-thon would be asking alumni for their "Time" to mentor students, and help other alumni get jobs. This is a perfect way to engage young alumni during the 10 years after graduation when their "Treasures" are being used to pay back their loans. Research is showing young alumni want to be engaged in helping their alma maters, but are turned off by the frequent requests for money during this period of their lives. This is an ideal way to give them a chance to participate.

I ran across a quote the other day that caught my attention and later saw it used on an ad on TV: *You can't prepare for the future while holding on to the past!*

The times, they are definitely changing.

The needs of your alumni are caught in the vortex of an uncertain employment market caused by political, social and worldwide competition. By focusing on your customers' needs, and delivering for them today, you set the stage for helping them build successful careers so they can support your college as it enters one of the most uncertain and competitive times of its history.

THE JURY IS IN! YOUR ALUMNI WANT HELP NETWORKING!

This is the number ONE requested service alumni want

Over the past year, TalentMarks has been busy introducing their CareerWebinars for Alumni series to alumni associations as a way to provide a "value added" services that help alumni build successful career strategies. Thousands of alumni have registered for the series that features the nation's top career authors and experts.

Designed on their successful CareerWebinars for Students series in which 1,000 career centers and 200,000 students participated, the CareerWebinars for Alumni series is built around a branded portal that includes the college logo, contact information and unique content.

Alumni directors love it because it's turnkey. TalentMarks does everything. Their staff books the guest speakers, sends out reminders, host the webinars, maintains and updates the portal, and provides clients analytics concerning participation. Even better, the speaker lineup is top notch!

For example, their fall line-up of speakers includes well known authors like Peter Weddle author of *Work Strong, Your Career Fitness Program*, Ben Casnocha who with Reid Hoffman, founder of LinkedIn, wrote *The StartUp of You*, and even Richard Bolles, author of the bestselling book of all times, What Color Is Your Parachute?

After each webinar this year, we surveyed alumni to get their ratings of the event, whether they would recommend it to others, and what they felt the most important messages were. We also found out in which additional areas they wanted the alumni association to provide help and guidance.

The five primary areas in which alumni requested help included:

1. Networking

2. Career coaching

3. Resumes

4. Career courses

5. Placement

The number one requested activity in all of our surveys was networking. This probably does not come as a surprise to anyone in alumni affairs as local surveys have more than likely shown a similar high interest in networking.

...but it got me thinking...

• How scalable is your ability to help alumni network?

• What percent of your alumni participate in networking events and activities?

• Are we getting mileage out of our online communities and LinkedIn pages?

• Do you have a way to measure how effective your events are for helping alumni network?

• Could we be doing a better job helping more alumni build their professional networks?

At live events, your alumni will be LUCKY if they make 2-3 contacts. Some of that is affected by the agenda and focus on the event, the rest by the fact that 60 percent of your alumni (according to the Stanford

Shyness Clinic) consider themselves shy. Shy people tend to lock on to one person at an event and there is a huge probability that person will not be in the same industry --so they *will not* be a prospective customer, nor will they be able to help advance the person in question's career.

A strong alumni association is a CONNECTED alumni association!

There is a side benefit to your alumni association having more connected alumni. According to Valdis Krebs, founder of Orgnet, organizations with members that are more connected are more engaged and involved in the mission of the group and the needs of its members. Valdis's firm provides social network analysis software & services for organizations, communities, and their consultants.

As alumni association's adoption of online communities were heating up a decade ago, Valdis shared with my clients the need to include a "gracious host" in their overall online community strategy. His research showed the value of having a more networked alumni base and he encouraged alumni directors to ACTIVELY connect alumni. His graphs and research helped us understand that alumni who are connected to each other strengthen and expand the network. A stronger network has the potential to help more students get internships, helps alumni do business with each other, helps alumni get jobs, and of course helps meet the needs of the college.

Unfortunately, since then, alumni online communities have become virtual ghost towns and are no longer viable strategies to network alumni. The good news is that they have been replaced by FREE solutions!

LinkedIn now has 250,000,000 users!

LinkedIn is a POWERFUL networking tool that few alumni associations are taking advantage of. Alumni participation is off the charts!

My alma mater has 196,000 alumni, and of those nearly 62,000 alumni have created a profile on LinkedIn. -- That's an astounding 31%! If every student created one LinkedIn profile, I predict that number would reach 45%.

LinkedIn offers a rich set of data that someone in the alumni office could use to match alumni. Wouldn't you like it if your alumni association periodically reached out to you and connected you with fellow alumni, or introduced you to an aspiring graduate who needed help in relocating to your area, or finding a job within your industry?

In the past year, LinkedIn has also introduced their www.linkedin/ alumni tool. This is a powerful, easy to use search tool that provides pre-selected data points to help users find people. With a click of the mouse, I can target people by:

- where they live

- what they do

- what they studied

- what they are skilled

- how I am connected to them

Your alumni association should teach every student and grad how to use this tool.

Consider focusing on recent grads: A survey by Addeco found that 29% of grads wished they had spent more time networking prior to graduation. Imagine how surprised and excited your recent grads will be when you reach out and help them build their professional networks!

Instead of investing staff time and attention on the abandoned and infrequently used alumni online community, consider redirecting your energies to data mining the vibrant and data rich online community of LinkedIn.

Facebook-- with a BILLION users-- has introduced their new Graph Search!

Another way you can take an active role in networking alumni is with Facebook. Facebook is slowly rolling out their new Graph Search to their billion users. This new search tool is pretty amazing! It enables users to do granular searches using simple phrases and sentences. We recently held a webinar that showed how job seekers could use it to network. For example, here are some searches I could do:

- Who of my friends' friends live in Chicago and work at IBM?

- Who graduated from Kent State University and works in advertising, in Los Angeles?

- Who graduated from Kent State University with a BS degree and works at Monsanto?

- Who graduated between X and Y years and majored in Journalism?

You could use this tool to strengthen your alumni network and help more alumni connect with one another. Someone in your office can search for graduates from a specific period, who received a bachelor's degree, who majored in (fill in the blank), who live in Los Angeles and work for Disney!

I could see a position dedicated to being a "gracious host" who spends his or her day, connecting alumni and building a stronger network of people who have a greater interest in helping each other.

Both Facebook and LinkedIn offer free online strategies to create a network that not only scales but gives you the opportunity to track the results and outcomes of your introductions.

If you'd like more details on how you can accomplish some of the ideas we've presented, reach out and let us know what you'd like to do!

3 WAYS TO HELP ALUMNI GET JOBS

*Help alumni build successful careers so
they can support campus needs*

We live in different times.

In 2007, over 50 percent of graduates had jobs by graduation day and another 12-19 percent went on to advanced degrees. Today, on a nationwide average, over 80 percent of graduates are unemployed the day their Dean or President hands their diplomas to them, and for grads that don't have a job by graduation day, it will take an average of 7.4 months to find one!

That's for graduates. What about alumni?

According to recent research the unemployment rate for alumni has doubled since 2007. <u>In fact, one report suggests 1 in 6 unemployed people have a bachelor's or higher degree.</u>

On top of those sobering statistics, The Department of Labor's research suggests those entering the workforce will have 10-14 jobs by the time they are 38 years old. Surveys suggest that looking for a job is among the top three stressful times in one's life, right up there with a death in a family and public speaking.

And looking for a job has changed enormously over the past 5 years! Most people 30 and older started their job searches by circling 140 character ads in the classifieds and then started calling those that sounded interesting. Today, when 6 people are trying to get every open position, job seekers have to be experts in Social Media, networking, interviewing and more!

So what can we do to help graduates and alumni?

We think colleges and universities have an enormous opportunity to help students and alumni lead more successful careers by:

• Making it part of their mission to deliver e-Learning career courses on networking, branding, how to find a job, how to use Social Media, interviewing techniques and much more!

• Deliver career services anytime, anywhere, through any device.

• Build stronger connections between faculty, students, alumni and the businesses they work for.

Research supports alumni want this!

In a research project for the American Insurance Administrators and the NEATrust, titled, "Current and Desired Relationship with Your Undergraduate Alma Mater" the Olson Zaltman Associates uncovered that alumni look at their alma mater for help, guidance and/or resources to help them in the transitions of their lives.

Using the patented interview and interpretation technique called the "Zaltman Metaphor Elicitation Technique," the researchers uncovered that:

• Alumni felt like they were just numbers to the college

• That the college was always asking but never giving value to them

• Alumni wanted the college to continue to provide the education, advice and resources they had as undergrads

The research suggested "Basically, universities must show that they have their alumni's best interests at heart." Alumni were looking to their alma mater for help in getting jobs and doing business, as well as help in financial matters like buying a home, car or even retiring. What they were not interested in was the "8 ways to give back to the college."

Focus on career and jobs!

Take a moment to reflect what your organization is doing to help grads and alumni. Are you:

1. Actively connecting alumni with similar interests to help build their professional networks?

2. Getting to know who they are and what issues they are dealing with at this point in their lives/careers?

3. Offering continued education that meets them where they are today?

More than likely, you don't have the time to focus on developing strategies to help alumni during all the transitions in their lives, but a great place to start is by using resources, connections, networks and opportunities to help alumni get jobs, do business and start businesses with each other!

Your alumni need help to build successful career strategies. Evaluate some of the ideas we discussed and get started today.

ANNUAL MENTORING CAMPAIGN!

Get more alumni committed and engaged to provide job shadowing
opportunities, internships and jobs for students and grads!

While watching a TED presentation as I worked out on my elliptical machine, my mind started to wander (as it frequently does) and I found myself thinking about fundraising.

Maybe it was the recent phone call from my alma mater, or perhaps the two letters from non-profits asking for donations, but I started to think about using annual giving fundraising techniques to increase the number of alumni who connect with, and mentor students.

As you know, and better than I, your annual giving team, cranks on their automated dialers in the fall and follows up on emails, post cards and letters asking alumni to support the needs of the college. If your college is like most, your annual giving department hires a team of students, or professionals to engage and talk with alumni about the wonderful things happening on campus and ask them to support the scholarship program.

Some are incredibly successful at this.

This is a list of the top six colleges with the highest percent of alumni participating in their annual giving program. Just look at their participation rates!

1.	Princeton University	62.2
2.	Thomas Aquinas	58.9
3.	Carlton College	58.2
4.	Williams College	57.5
5.	Amherst College	57.3
6.	Centre College	54.9

Pretty impressive isn't it?

That got me thinking about the three "T's" --a phrase I heard while attending nearly one hundred CASE conferences over 12 years.

People give their Time, Treasure or Talent!

While the above colleges have phenomenal numbers of alumni who are contributing their "treasure" to their annual giving program, they must have an equal number who would be willing to give their "time and talent" if a meaningful opportunity was available that fit into their busy lifestyles.

So that got me thinking...

Why not have an annual mentoring campaign in the spring where the annual giving team would be temporarily reassembled to call alumni and ask them to be "active" mentors to incoming freshmen? Experience will tell us which former students are going to be the best prospects. Perhaps it's alumni who have graduated in the past 5 years, because they still remember the tips and techniques they learned the hard way to advance their careers. Maybe it's boomers who are near retirement who have decades of experience, knowledge and contacts, or perhaps it's alumni who were part of clubs and organizations on campus.

Imagine how easy it would be to get alumni to participate if your callers said something like this:

"Hi (name), I wanted to reach out to you to let you know we have adopted a new program for incoming freshman where we partner them with an alum who can mentor them, offer advice and perhaps introduce them to other alumni that might be able to help them get job shadowing opportunities, internships or even jobs.   As you know it's a tough job market for students today.   Our research is showing students with internships are not only getting jobs at a higher rate, but also higher pay.   Would you be willing to look at information that outlines how you can be an official (mascot name) mentor?"

Whether you have 300 or 3,000 incoming freshman, it should be relatively easy to make this happen! What if you had even 10 percent of your alumni volunteering to mentor, provide job shadowing experiences and making commitments to provide internships and jobs for students and grads?   That could easily guarantee that each freshman had a mentor!

Getting started is easy!

1. Write up a one page proposal outlining how you want to use the Annual Giving Fundraising Team to run a Spring Annual Mentoring Campaign.

2. Develop a simple way to match and introduce students.   It might even be something as simple as introducing them via LinkedIn or an email.

3. Meet with the Development and Annual Giving teams to share the idea with them.

As much as we'd like it, no new program runs completely on it's on. It will take some time to organize your first year campaign, as well as to develop an automated system to make sure that students and mentors are connecting, but the long term benefits will be phenomenal.

If I were you, I'd also create an outline of what the mentors are supposed to do. Give them a "Job Description" that includes their responsibilities and what they are accountable for. In that job description, I would encourage them to remind students to be taking ownership of their careers as well as visiting the career center.

I could envision a time where every student coming on your campus is assigned not one, but multiple mentors who will act as a support group for the student during his or her entire college experience. And, I could see, as long as the student did what was required, this team would do everything in their power to make sure that student had a job by graduation day!

This program could result in more grads getting jobs by graduation day, then any other activity. And the great thing about it is, once it's up and running, it should run itself!

"If your actions inspire others to dream more, learn more, do more and become more, you are a leader."

John Quincy Adams

9 WHO SHOULD BE LEADING THIS CHANGE?

In this section we'll look at administrative and government policy with an eye on who should be leading this change and what responsibilities everyone has.

You know what you need to do today to help your graduates, but you will need the support and engagement of everyone to make it a reality. You will have to go to the top to make sure the bridges you build to other departments stay connected and that everyone is singing from the same hymnal.

Let's examine who should be leading the culture change on your campus.

Here are the 7 topics we'll discuss:

1. Career center Directors Know How To Fix Grad Unemployment, But Administrators Are Not Listening!

2. College Requires Community Service - But NOT Career Study!

3. "An Open Letter to College Presidents", Is BAD News for Career Services

4. Rutgers University Fired The Wrong Guy!

5. What is your College President FOCUSED on?

6. Your College Does Not Have to Go Out Of Business Like Newspapers Are

7. Will President Obama Help GRADS Get Jobs?

1

CAREER CENTER DIRECTORS KNOW HOW TO FIX GRAD UNEMPLOYMENT, BUT ADMINISTRATORS ARE NOT LISTENING!

Find innovative ways to get management's attention

Another 1,700,000 graduates are hitting the streets this summer, each looking for a dream job and a chance to start a professional life.

All seem to be aware, but most do not admit, that they are in competition for jobs with not only their fellow graduates, but the 8 million unemployed, 7 million underemployed, and --some say-- 5 million people that have stopped actively looking for a job.

All have high hopes, but few are aware that it takes the average grad nearly 8 months to find a job. That's unfortunate! A grad with a job immediately after graduation that pays $15 per hour earns enough in 8 months to nearly pay off his or her student loans! In a previous blog post I shared that the Class of 2013 will collectively lose out *on $50 BILLION dollars* in salary!

It doesn't have to be that way!

With the right knowledge, skills and focus, I'm convinced more grads could have jobs lined up by graduation day.

...and there are plenty of studies to prove it. NACE has conducted surveys and found that students who invest time in career development and who visit the career center not only get internships, but are more likely to have jobs lined up, in their fields of study, at higher pay!

Other studies have been trying to get management's attention!

There are a half a dozen reports by organizations like the Pew Research Center's Internet & American Life Project, Adecco, HERI, John J. Heldrich Center for Workforce Development and the Associated Press that have identified issues college graduates are facing; however, little is being done at the executive level to solve the problems.

These reports, and others, seem to have fallen on deaf ears as upper management's response has been to cut career centers' budgets. In fact, in the past year, according to NACE surveys, the average career center budget was slashed 15%!

In an effort to help administrations understand these issues and share solutions with management, the Career Advisory Board surveyed nearly 600 career center directors.

Its recommendations?

1. Require career courses.

2. Cultivate relationships with faculty to promote career exploration and management.

3. Move the career center to higher traffic areas.

4. Hire student ambassadors.

5. Hire more staff.

6. Work with third party providers.

I'm not sure why those studies have not encouraged the president's committee to invest more and put a greater focus on careers on campus but the reality is that a generation of grads is being dumped on the streets to "find their its own way."

What has baffled me is that only a handful of colleges are providing their career centers with the resources and authority to act on these recommendations. Each year, despite all the bad news about unemployed and underemployed grads, in reckless ignorance, college administrations continue to ignore the issue.

Sooner or later, a perfect storm of grad unemployment, underemployment, and price pressure from low cost online educations, along with a more savvy prospective customer base is going to wake up the president's round table.

I hope you can get the ear of your president before it's too late!

COLLEGE REQUIRES COMMUNITY SERVICE - BUT NOT CAREER STUDY!

Your college COULD require students to invest 20-40 hours in career study before they graduate

Article suggests college require students invest minimum time in career planning:

In the mid to late 90's, high schools and colleges had a huge upswing in administration mandating students to complete a specific number of "community service" hours in order to graduate.

There was a general "group think" among community leaders, administrators, and legislatures that requiring students to participate in community service projects would help introduce them to the value of giving back, while at the same time it would be a good way they could repay the community for subsidizing their educations.

In Nassau County, New York, the Roslyn and Hewlett-Woodmere districts approved a program that required students, beginning with the class of 1997, to take a one-semester, half-credit, community-service course and to complete a minimum of 30 hours of field work to graduate. (This was raised to 40 hours for the next class.) A neighboring county, Suffolk, instituted a similar program. Then Superintendent John G. Barnes was quoted to say, "We believe that community service is a must

259

for all students."

These experiments in developing mandated community service programs at the local level bubbled up to the state level.

In 1997, the state of Maryland instituted a statewide mandatory community service high school graduation requirement. The law stipulated that students who attend public high schools complete a minimum of 75 community service hours.

A student reflected on first hearing about this requirement at a school assembly.

"I heard our principal say - Look to your left, look to your right. I guarantee some of you won't graduate because of the community service requirement. You can be a 4.0 student and get into any college you want, but you won't graduate because of the community service requirement."

The student's first reaction? "Whoa, they are serious about this!"

Even without mandated community service programs, as the admissions process to college became more competitive, students were advised to complete community service in order to improve their chances of being admitted.

As a result of political, cultural, and legislative focus on community service, the number of college students who participated in community services while in high school has steadily increased over the past two decades. According to the Cooperative Intuitional Research Program, about one-third of first-year college students graduated from high schools with some type of requirement for service.

Most colleges embraced community service as a founding principal of their college. Harvard and Yale were founded to educate missionaries who could spread out into the distant areas of the growing United States and carry the Presbyterian message. The College of William and Mary was founded to produce graduates that could minister to Indians and attempt to convert them to Christianity.

Look at the missions of almost any college and you will see community service being a core part of the college culture. Some, over time, like the high schools, mandated community service hours in order for students to graduate.

- Tougaloo College requires students, by graduation, to complete 60 hours of community service that is approved by the chair of their departments.

- Mercy College of Health Sciences requires students to complete a 20-hour community service project. The project includes volunteering and submitting a report about their activities. There is no grade or credit provided.

- Southern University in Louisiana, a public university, requires 60 hours of community service in order to graduate. The college has actually created community service classes that teach community engagement.

- Liberty University has required community service of their students since it was founded and offers students over 350 different locations for students to volunteer. They also require students to complete two single hour community service classes their first year of full time enrollment.

- The University of Redlands requires students to take a 3-unit service activity course that places students in programs focused on homeless shelters, pre-schools, police departments, safe-havens and various other nonprofit agencies. Each year students invest over 60,000 hours in these programs

Other colleges may not require students to commit a specific number of community service volunteer hours, but do their best to provide channels and build enthusiasm for community service.

- Loyola College offers students the Loyola4Chicago program as one of many channels to volunteer. Students agree to spend 4 hours a week in service teams at various sites, including working with children, immigrants, and people with mental illness, as well as people experiencing homelessness and others.

- Eastern Connecticut State University offers students regular events that build camaraderie and positive community experiences through their Poverty Marathon and Day of Giving events.

- George Washington University organizes an annual Freshman Day of Service. The event focus changes from year to year but immediately indoctrinates students into a culture of giving back to the community. It's not unusual for GWU students to spend over 160,000 hours a year volunteering.

- Stanford University dedicates 22.3 percent of its work study funds toward programs that help the community and society in general. Program dollars support autism awareness and bringing dance to prisoners, as well as greening up South African schools.

- San Francisco State University, like many universities, has a department dedicated to raising awareness of community service. Their Institute for Civic and Community Engagement, has over 7,000 students enrolled in its Community Service Learning program, which blends service projects with course work in order to educate and stimulate a culture of "giving back" to the community.

- Willamette University's Office of Community Service Learning provides a database of 250 charities and causes for students to participate in. Students have enthusiastically responded by investing 150,000 hours of community service work.

- Lee University takes a different tack and offers course credit to students who participate in or create volunteer opportunities.

- To increase awareness and participation in community service, Ohio Wesleyan University makes heroes of students who rack up the most volunteer hours. Each year, they host the "Golden Bishops" ceremony that awards students who have been the most philanthropically engaged.

- North Carolina State University had over 21,000 students spend 330,000 hours during 2010 and 2011 helping serve disadvantaged youth and support early childhood literacy.

- Seattle University's administration made $50,000 available for college faculty and staff to implement projects and engage volunteers to support community projects.

While some might speculate that requiring students to participate in community service programs would in fact generate negative feelings towards the concept of giving back to the community, surveys indicate otherwise. Liberty University conducted a survey to determine if they should continue to require students to fulfill a community service requirement in order to graduate.

- Seventy percent supported the requirement to commit volunteer in community service projects.

- Seventy six percent said they had a positive attitude about performing the required community service.

- There were a variety of reasons students offered why they participated which ranged from, helping people to feeling good about themselves and improving the community, as well as (a small minority) improving their resumes.

To help colleges and universities advance their strategies and operate as a clearing house of best practices and resources, a national organization called Campus Compact was founded in 1985 by Brown, Georgetown and Stanford Universities.

<u>There are currently 1,200 dues-paying colleges and universities with college members that represent over 6 million students. </u> The program reaches to the highest level of the university, the presidents, to help drive the message through their cultures and continues to support the initiatives and events that drive student engagement in volunteer programs.

In fact, Campus Compact developed a statement of purpose it asks the presidents of its member institutions to agree to. The President's Declaration on Civic Responsibility of Higher Education offers a foundation for the organization and presidents' commitments to community engagement. In the President's Statement of Principles, the first principle highlights their commitments:

Campus Compact presidents strongly advocate the participation of students, faculty, staff, and higher education institutions in public and community service. Such service may range from individual acts of student volunteerism to institution-wide efforts to improve the social and economic well-being of America's communities.

And it works!

The total value of service contributed by students at Campus Compact member schools is estimated to be over 7 billion dollars based on the 377 million volunteer service hours contributed each year.

So why did I cover so much detail here?

I hope I didn't lose you in all the detail and information shared on colleges' and universities' commitments to community service. The practices and college commitments are admirable and necessary. The students who donate the hours and are the backbone of the program are to be commended for their participation, regardless of whether it is required,

My goal in giving you all of this detail is to show how embedded in the college culture the concept of community service is. In the example above I shared:

1. Colleges that set specific hours required for students to graduate

2. Organizations that provide funding to support new initiatives and staffing for volunteer projects

3. Departments funded on campus with names like Community Service Outreach, supported by student activity funds

4. Administrators at the highest level who are active participants in promulgating the culture

While volunteerism is important, in my opinion, the career center and career development should be at the center of the college experience. Everything a student does, every club, organization, work-study program, course and activity should tie in – in some manner to the relevance to the end game, giving grads the practical skills to search for and get jobs--a process they will likely go through 20 or more times in their lives.

I'd like to see the presidents of all colleges and universities to do as they did when they joined Campus Compact and sign a President's Declaration of Commitment to Career Planning and Management. That declaration would signal the importance the president places on increasing the number of grads who get jobs within their career fields of choice and get jobs by --or soon after-- graduation day.

You can help this happen. Contact your college administrators and ask them to participate. Let us know if we can offer any help!

"AN OPEN LETTER TO COLLEGE PRESIDENTS", IS BAD NEWS FOR CAREER SERVICES

Foreword thinking commitment by leading Presidents doesn't mention a focus on career management

On an unusually cold April weekend, when I should have been out riding 20 miles on my bike, I ended up settling into a comfortable old leather chair to read a report issued by the National Commission on Higher Education Attainment (NCHEA) that was titled, An Open Letter to College and University Leaders: College Completion Must Be Our Priority.

Apparently, the Obama administration asked the American Council of Education (ACE) to convene a group of college and university presidents to discuss steps colleges and universities could take to increase the number of Americans who complete college. The ACE pulled together 6 presidential associations from Washington, DC who reached out to college presidents willing to serve on the new committee.

Based on the pedigree of the organizations behind the report and their membership base, it was clear to me that what I was about to read reflected the thinking of presidents at colleges and universities across America and it would guide the investment of resources, both staff and money, for the next decade. After reading:

"We believe every institution must pay as much attention to the number of degrees it grants— completion—as it does to success in admissions and recruitment. It is now time for all colleges and universities to marshal the resources needed to make completion our strategic priority."

...I was hoping to see the report recommend an emphasis on, and a commitment to career services.

Unfortunately, after reading the report twice, I couldn't find any indication that the commission was going to suggest colleges and universities emphasize career exploration, career planning and career development as a way to increase the number of students that graduate.

The report suggested there were three broad categories colleges and universities could focus on that would increase the number of students that graduate:

• Changing campus culture to boost student success

• Improving cost-effectiveness and quality

• Making better use of data to boost success

I was hopeful that the first category would suggest that colleges focus on career planning like I wrote about in my report, Create a career centered College Culture and Campus. As I dug into, "Changing campus culture to boost student success," I slowly digested the key points:

1. Assign ownership of this process to someone

2. Implement initiative campus-wide

3. Suggest colleges study past mistakes

4. Create a student-centered culture

5. Improve the academic experience

6. Give credit for previous learning

7. Provide support services for nontraditional students

8. Teach the teachers

As I wiggled in my chair, I kept thumbing through the 30 page report trying to find comments that might have to do with career services. The only place I found a brief statement about career services was in a paragraph about Fairleigh Dickinson University's nationally recognized veterans career support programs. So I reexamined the report to see if there was a veiled mention, or implied reference that would suggest campuses emphasize career development. I went back into the above points and zeroed in on numbers 2, 4 and 7 hoping I would see a suggestion to college presidents to put an emphasis on career education and training.

But, alas, there was none!

It was at that moment, that I realized that career services is just not on the radar of college presidents. It was at that moment, that I realized college presidents do not see that a focus on careers could increase retention, graduation rate and the number of grads with jobs!

There should be no doubt in your mind that this is indeed an important report that will effect change on your campus! The President of Ohio State University, E. Gordon Gee's, introductory letter offers a call to action for college presidents:

"Most important, this letter is a renewed call for collective and immediate action at a pivotal moment for higher education. We must make bold decisions and seize opportunities, we must do it now, and we must do it together. We ask for your help and commitment to ensuring a bright future for higher education."

This initiative, called for by the Obama administration, is going to get a great deal of attention on your campus over the next decade, However, unless you speak up, your career center is not going to be included in this movement. The good news is you have a unique opportunity to use this report to raise awareness about the importance of career exploration, development and management on your campus.

To do that, I'd suggest you write a one page outline of how your department can increase retention and the number of students that graduate. Then paper clip it, along with a cover letter, and a copy of the NCHEA report, and give it to your boss, or hand it directly to the president.

In your one page report:

- Compare how much your campus is spending per student on career services, versus other departments, AND include campuses you regard as leaders in this area.

- Share stats and information conducted by NACE that prove that students who invest more time in their careers will not only get internships but jobs by graduation day.

- Identify what you want to do, but currently can't, because of staffing and budget issues.

- Share stats, like the UCLA, HERI Freshman Survey that prove students are going to college to get a better job, as well as stats by Adeco, Heldrich and Pew that suggest grads wished they spent more time on career development.

- Make sure your president is aware that this is an institutional problem nationwide by sharing the Career Advisory Boards report that suggested nearly 50 percent of career center directors don't think grads have what it takes to find a job!

- Share how an emphasis on careers will increase retention, the graduation rate and the number of grads with jobs.

You have an incredible opportunity to get the ear of your president and get the resources you think you need, as well as begin to change the culture on campus to focus on careers.

However, if you don't take this opportunity right now, I can guarantee you will continue to struggle to make a difference in the lives of students who don't take ownership of their career because the campus is not focused on career exploration, development and management.

You must seize the opportunity Gordon Gee mentions and make this moment, your moment on your campus! <u>Be a part of this discussion and movement!</u>

RUTGERS UNIVERSITY FIRED THE WRONG GUY!

Why not fire someone who is responsible for
grads NOT getting jobs!?

I really got mad the other day after watching the TV show Morning Joe.

Morning Joe hosts Joe Scarborough, Mika Brezezinski, Willie Geist and their guests were talking about the firing of Mike Rice, the head basketball coach of Rutgers University, for being abusive to the players.

Apparently, a video tape was shared with Tim Pernetti, the Rutgers athletic director about 5 months earlier, that showed Rice pushing, shoving, grabbing, cursing, throwing balls at the players, and using abusive gay-slurring language. (Sound like a couple bosses you've had?)

While it has been reported that the highly edited tapes represented only 1/2 of one percent of the time Rice had spent coaching the team, nonetheless, they made him look like an angry, out of control, homophobic cave man. The athletic director did the right thing and immediately ordered an investigation, brought in attorneys to interview the players, and examined the university's exposure to lawsuits. In a relatively short period of time, Pernetti suspended the basketball coach for 3 games and fined him $50,000. Case closed right? Hardly!

Nearly 6 months later, the video tape was posted on YouTube and caught the eye of ESPN, other media outlets and talk shows like Morning

Joe, nearly all that faulted the administration for letting the situation happen, not doing enough to prevent it, or not doing enough to rectify it.

Cries to fire the athletic director and president

The hosts and guests on Morning Joe were suggesting the athletic director should be fired and even speculated the president must have known about it and should be held accountable. Within 2 days the athletic director was fired and now I'm seeing articles calling for the president to resign!

So why did this bug me?

First of all, in my opinion, the college handled the situation in a transparent way. The athletic director took the situation seriously, attorneys were brought in, the players were interviewed, and the coach was reprimanded. It's easy to second guess situations in hindsight, but I do give credit to the athletic director for facing the issues and reprimanding the coach. At least he did something!

What bugs me is that this situation has the media, legislatures, and alumni around the world talking.

What bugs me is to see everyone obsessing on an issue that affected only 18 players, yet, in just a few weeks, 5,000+ Rutgers grads will be receiving their diplomas, and another 1,700,000 grads around the country will receive their hard earned diplomas from their deans and presidents and ....

...these grads will be leaving college with an average of $27,000 in debt, while having invested upwards to $100,000 in family and personal savings to get a degree, while at the same time racking up over $5,000 in credit card debt. Worse, based on a NACE study, it will take the average grad nearly 8 months to find a job, losing out on $24,000 in salary!

And yet, no one at the college is doing anything to change this situation.

Could one argue that the college is taking advantage of students and pushing them off the commencement stage into a world they are totally unprepared for? Is the college doing anything to help grads in their first professional job searches so they don't end up being bullied by student loan debt collectors?

Ironically, the John J. Heldrich Center for Workforce Development Center at Rutgers University, issued a report issued two years ago entitled, Unfulfilled Expectations: Recent College Graduates Struggle in a Troubled Economy . The report asked grads, "How well did your college education prepare you to look for a full time job?" The result...

- 24% reported - Not Well at All

- 24% reported - Not Very Well (looks repetitive, but that's how they worded it!)

It also reported that 40% were working in jobs that did not require a college degree.

Career center professionals don't think grads are ready for their first professional job searches either. The Career Advisory Board Survey of 600 career professionals showed that:

- 48.1% thought students did not have the knowledge they needed to find jobs

- 55.7% felt students resumes were not professional enough to use for their job searches

Can anyone tell me of a college administration that is pulling together a task force, bringing in the attorneys, talking to the career center professionals, to come up with solutions to the situations college graduates are facing today?

So if Joe, Mika, Willie and guests think the athletic director, and possibly the president, should be fired over this situation, who should be fired because a significant number of the 8,000 Rutgers grads of the Class of 2013 fail to get a job after college? <u>Who should be fired because the they are ignoring a generation of graduates who are becoming indentured servants to the organizations that own their student loans?</u>

We are all responsible!

- First of all, parents are responsible for not raising the importance of this issue to college administrators and demanding they invest more resources in the career center and better prepare their sons or daughters for the college to corporate transition.

- Students need to take ownership of their careers the minute they get on campus. Career development is a marathon, not a sprint that is completed in the final weeks of college.

- Alumni should be doing more to provide mentoring and internships and to hire graduates. Every college has enough alumni with businesses that could hire graduates.

- Faculty should be supporting career center initiatives that require students to spend time evaluating career opportunities and creating their career plans.

- Instead of focusing on basketball stats, college administrators should be focusing on stats that show more students are getting jobs by graduation day and implementing strategies that will improve those stats!

Hillary Clinton in her book It Takes A Village suggested everyone in the community was responsible for raising youth. In this case, the entire campus community, including parents and alumni, are responsible for helping more grads get jobs by graduation day, and students need to spend time each month at the career center to pick up the skills and knowledge they will need to get jobs.

It's time we all started obsessing about grads' needs or someone is going to end up getting fired!

WHAT IS YOUR COLLEGE PRESIDENT FOCUSED ON?

Fundraising, Construction, Admissions, Retention?

I recently attended a pre-homecoming luncheon for a large state college where the president of the university gave a short pep talk about the improvements and changes that are happening on campus.

As you know, my focus, my sole interest is that we find ways to help more grads have jobs on graduation day, so when the president rolled into a rapid fire litany of improvements, I was looking for some direction and clues as to what his cabinet's plan was to increase the percent of grads with jobs on graduation day.

So I waited.

I heard how the college was investing hundreds of millions of dollars on rehabbing buildings on campus and how a number of buildings were already upgraded to state of the art facilities that "our students deserve." The president talked about a strong new partnership with the community which was building a bridge to the town to create a whole new experience for students and alumni and would more importantly to revitalize the town.

Then I heard him talk about the incredible success the college had, of course with the support of alumni, to raise hundreds of millions of dollars for the university so the university can fund scholarships for students.

With a great deal of pride, the president shared how the college had become the second largest college in the state and that their admissions team is continuing to work hard to build on the positive buzz about alumni success, the renovations, new programs added to the college, and the success of the sports program.

Then, finally I heard the president talk about increasing retention of students and doing everything he could do to make sure students graduate on time.

As he ended his presentation, we were challenged to go back to work and make a lot of money to help support the needs of the college. (Unfortunately it was a beautiful Friday afternoon and I had already planned to take a bike ride!)

To be honest, I was impressed with the progress the relatively new president and his team had made. The physical campus was reaching a mature level that gave it a luster and "class" that was missing. It was becoming a place that was sure to attract students, make alumni proud, and keep it higher in national admissions rankings.

However, what I came to hear, what I wanted him to share - was that he was going to invest more resources in the career center, and focus next on increasing the number of grads with jobs on graduation day. That didn't happen.

So what does your president focus on?

- Fundraising?

- Building out the infrastructure?

- Increasing enrollment?

- Improving retention?

Your president is more than likely focusing on things that he/she and the board feel are critical for your college. At this point in time, students are not complaining to the administration that the college is not doing enough to prepare them for their first professional job searches. Parents who are stuck with a huge loan to pay off are not sending letters, emails or calling and complaining. Even the media and government for the time being are giving the college some slack and not asking them to provide a plan. Until somebody does, I'm afraid the president, his administration and board will not pay attention to the plight of their graduates - AND alumni!

That's where YOU can help!

The recent survey by CAB indicates:

- 55.4 percent of career professionals don't think grads' resumes are ready for prime time

- 48.1 percent don't think grads are ready for their first professional job searches.

- So if you agree, you need to find ways to get the president's help to do something about it!

- Your job is to remind him or her about your students' and grads' needs.

- Try to find ways to get your message across to your boss. See if you can engage students who are committed to career exploration to become more vocal about their needs. Make a commitment for 2014 that you will get your president focused on helping more grads get jobs!

YOUR COLLEGE DOES NOT HAVE TO GO OUT OF BUSINESS LIKE NEWSPAPERS ARE

Focus on getting grads jobs and admissions can charge whatever the market will bear!

College presidents and the presidents of newspapers around the country have something in common: every week, someone is bringing to their attention that their business model is in jeopardy.

In a book I wrote in 2006 (Internet Dough) to help small businesses understand the value of social media, I included a chapter about how the Internet was disintermediating businesses. I shared tips and ideas about how small business owners could bypass traditional advertising channels like newspapers, and create their own marketing channels by adopting, then emerging social media tools and services.

At the time, most newspapers were enjoying a huge 20 percent net profit; yet their leaders understood the Internet poised a risk to their business models.

While the brightest marketers, CEO's, and leaders frantically threw everything including the kitchen sink at the problem, the only thing they could do to maintain profitability was to cut costs. And cut costs they did! Each year, they slashed staff and overhead and renegotiated contracts with unions. Yet, that was not enough! The disintermediating effect of the Internet forced the Tucson Citizen, Rocky Mountain News, Baltimore Examiner, Kentucky Post, Cincinnati Post, King County Journal, Union City Register-Tribune, Halifax Daily News, Albuquerque Tribune, South Idaho Press and many more to shut down!

Now, 7 years later my hometown newspaper, The Cleveland Plain Dealer, once Ohio's largest newspaper, has introduced a once unthinkable strategy of moving to delivering the paper to consumers only 3 days a week!   This is a newspaper that --less than 20 years ago-- would be bought by Al Neuharth, then CEO of Gannett Company for 1/2 a billion dollars, and today would be lucky to be get $40 million dollars in a sale.

Your college president is facing the same issues!

While leaders in the newspaper industry have been preparing for this for the past decade, college presidents are only recently being tasked by their board to show they understand the risk, and are doing something about it.

Only recently the board of trustees for The University of Virginia abruptly brought this to the attention of college presidents worldwide when they fired their president, Teresa Sullivan, for not implementing changes fast enough to keep pace with the disintermediating effects of online learning, and changing consumer behaviors.

My son recently shared with me an article by Mark Cuban, owner of the Dallas Mavericks, titled, Will your College Go Out of Business Before You Graduate? In his blog post, Mark outlines why colleges and universities will face the same issues and fate the newspaper industry has painfully endured. (Mark doesn't offer much hope for your job, but stay with me as I'm going to outline why this is the best thing that could happen to you!)

So why is Mark warning prospective students that your college could go out of business?

Your college has probably not seen fat profits like the newspaper industry has, but like the newspaper industry--more than likely--

your college has racked up a lot of debt in order to staff competitively, add amenities, spruce up the campus, add new departments/majors, courses, clubs, and expand the physical campus.

This debt will require your college to continue to increase the cost of tuition, at a time that congress is making student loans harder to get and when states are drastically cutting higher education funding. A perfect storm is brewing!

These market force changes combined with the disintermediating effect of the Internet, the changing behaviors of consumers, and the acceptance of online education, will create a situation that will undoubtedly require administrators to make drastic changes in staffing, course offerings and services.

Discussions are already underway in Texas. The nine regents that oversee the university system, all appointed by Governor Rick Perry, want the universities to figure out how to offer students a four-year degree for a total of $10,000 in tuition!

You may not be facing this, but I guarantee your president will be forced to implement a strategy to slash costs, cut staff, and reduce overhead in a draconian process to protect the institution and integrity of the diploma awarded to tens of thousands of alumni!

Don't believe your college could go out of business?

Research conducted by Richard Kneedler, President Emeritus of Franklin & Marshall College, way back in 2007, even before the debilitating effects of the economic crash, provided a very detailed analysis of the state of higher education borrowing. His analysis showed that 207 colleges had more debt than assets - which put them at risk if their enrollment suddenly dropped or lenders got skittish. He suggested that as many as one third of all colleges could be at risk because their revenues no longer supports their debts.

An article by Nathan Harden in The American Interest paints an even worse picture for your college in the next half century!

In fifty years, if not much sooner, half of the roughly 4,500 colleges and universities now operating in the United States will have ceased to exist. The technology driving this change is already at work, and nothing can stop it. The future looks like this: Access to college-level education will be free for everyone; the residential college campus will become largely obsolete; tens of thousands of professors will lose their jobs; the bachelor's degree will become increasingly irrelevant; and ten years from now Harvard will enroll ten million students.

And, check out what Blaire Briody has to say in an article of The Week, titled, Why Your College Could Go Bankrupt

Moody's Investors Service recently gave a negative outlook to all U.S. universities, citing "mounting fiscal pressure on all key university revenue sources," as a number of states continue to cut higher education budgets, endowments fall, and enrollment numbers and tuition dollars dwindle. Long-term debt at not-for-profit universities has been growing at 12 percent a year, according to consulting firm Bain & Company and private-equity firm Sterling Partners.

Keep in mind this is before taking into effect the debilitating market forces we discussed earlier and changing consumer behaviors.

Your college has to show your value proposition!

"We know the model is not sustainable," said Lawrence T. Lesick, vice president for enrollment management at Ohio Northern University. "Schools are going to have to show the value proposition. <u>Those that don't aren't going to be around."</u>

Lawrence T. Lesick is right!

Think about how you buy products and services.

Imagine for a moment that you are at your neighborhood Lowes and you are shopping for a washer and dryer. You have a price range in which you are looking know you want a front loader washer. The sales person shows you the models they have, and even though she is aware of the top end you are willing to spend, introduces you to a model that has higher efficiency, uses less hot water, less soap, is more environmentally friendly, and has a longer guarantee--but it's $200 more then you are willing to spend. The manufacturer was prepared for your price resistance, and educated the sales person to show you how you will recoup the $200 investment during the first year of use in reduced electricity costs and soap costs. Plus, the sales person reminds you of the advanced features you will enjoy for the next 10 years as well as the fact that you will be a "friend to the environment"!

In order to stay competitive, your college needs to immediately evaluate how you can deliver a return on investment to your students. Management is going to need to show prospective students and their parents why they should be DELIGHTED to pay your tuition!

So how will you do that?

Simple! By proving that student who choose you have a better chance of graduating with a job.

Your administrators are going to have to pull together the entire campus community; faculty, staff, alumni and your department to create a strategy that increases:

1. students taking ownership of their career and investing time in career exploration, planning and management;

2. the number of students with internships; and

3. the number of grads with jobs by graduation day!

It's really that simple!

By showing your customers that your product will provide them a better return on investment then online colleges and alternative learning channels, you will be able to maintain your costs, increase enrollment, and save the jobs of colleagues in your department and every department on campus!

You will have a voice in the changes that are coming, as long as you step forward and offer solutions. I wish you luck as you help lead your college through the disintermediating forces you face today!

WILL PRESIDENT OBAMA HELP GRADS GET JOBS?

The government needs to provide incentives
to students and graduates.

Is the student loan portfolio too BIG to fail? The default rate increased from 6.7% to 13.8% in 4 years!

The facts:

• The student loan portfolio is now approaching one trillion dollars, a point someone is going to suggest is "Too big to fail."

• 80 percent of grads since 2008 did not have jobs the days their presidents or deans handed their diplomas to them.

The default rate on student loans has doubled in just four years, putting hundreds of billions of dollars in student loans in default already. The problem is not going to go away. This year, as in previous years, colleges and universities produced over 1,700,000 graduates (85% in May and June), yet the economy is producing under 75,000 new jobs each month.

College presidents, President Obama, and our nation's leaders <u>need to understand there is a lot of pain in those numbers for students and families who trusted these institutions</u> and literally mortgaged their lives to get degrees.

• Grads' careers are being delayed and their income potential will likely be stunted for life.

- Parents and grads are burdened with huge loan payments reducing their abilities to make purchases.

- <u>Damaged credit ratings will prevent grads from getting jobs!</u>

- Marriages are delayed or take place due to huge student loans.

- Grads are working in careers totally unrelated to their degrees.

We have an enormous amount of talented, educated grads from the finest institutions in the world that are living in their parents' basements and pouring coffee or tending bar to pick up spare change.

I would suggest Congress, colleges, and organizations work together to find a way to give meaningful internships and employment to college and continue to help these students even after they graduate. I'd love to see a national PAID Internship program that marshals the support of businesses, non-profits, religious organizations, state/local governments, and alumni.

A nationwide solution would utilize the Internet to connect organizations to students willing to work.

Students could be employed by these organizations to:

1. develop and manage social media programs for small business from Betty's Beauty Parlor to mid-sized and Fortune 500 companies

2. handle overflow customer service chats, emails, or phone calls

3. conduct polls and research and write blog articles

4. take inbound sales calls or make outbound sales calls

College Presidents could start in their own back yards by implementing strategies to make this happen. For instance, they could:

- Assign alumni mentors to incoming freshman - BEFORE they arrive on campus.

- Require students to take a career exploration courses and learn networking and job search techniques during their four years on campus.

- In addition to asking for contributions, challenge alumni to get their organizations to hire an Intern.

Legislatures need to develop programs that will:

1. Provide tax breaks to companies providing PAID student internships

2. Offer tax breaks on income earned by Interns

3. Offer "Student Loan Credits" to students who work at reduced rates

4. Build excitement and encourage participation in a national program

Students can't solve this problem!

Our colleges, government, and lending institutions created this problem. It will require the leadership of our college presidents, businesses, and congressional leaders to implement cost effective solutions to not only rescue troubled lives, but to shore up a shaky loan program and perhaps save the higher education industry itself.

There is a WIN-WIN situation out there if leadership is willing to put aside differences and think creatively.

This is a "Too Big To Fail" situation!

The cost is too high to ignore it; the pain is only going to get worse. Do you have the leadership to step up to this challenge?

"Success consists of going from one failure to another without loss of enthusiasm."

- Winston Churchill

10 MOVING TO A "CAREER CENTERED" CULTURE

Hillary Clinton in her book, *It Takes A Village*, reminded us that we are all responsible for bringing up our children. It's the responsibility of the parents, the baker, plumber, congressperson, doctor, in addition to our teachers and court systems to provide a safe and nurturing environment that will help our children transition to responsible adults.

Based on the conversations I've had with career professionals, they believe that every administrator, faculty and staff as well as parents are responsible for getting students from their first freshman class to their first job.

And I agree!

Every department on campus has some responsibility in ensuring that students graduate and lead fulfilling lives and careers.

This series of mini-chapters and discussion will examine new trends, issues and strategies you need to consider as you move your college down this path. This is no small task but it is a necessary one, that someone has to spearhead and lead.

And I'm hoping that will be you!

Here are the 7 topics we'll discuss:

1. Do Careers Get Enough Focus On Your Campus?

2. It Takes a Campus to Build a Successful Career!

3. University of Phoenix Builds College Culture Around Career

Exploration & Management

4. Who Are Your Customers? Students or the Companies That Hire Them?

5. Are You Doing Enough To Help Students Choose Their Career Paths?

6. What are Your Plans to Increase the Number of Career Center Visits?

7. Require - Make - Demand Students Invest Time In Their Careers

1

DO CAREERS GET ENOUGH FOCUS ON YOUR CAMPUS?

Mandatory participation in groups and activities prevents students from investing time in career planning and management

 In doing research for my book The Employed Grad, Skills, Knowledge and Information Your Grad Will Need to Get a Job, I spent some time explaining to parents why colleges have not historically been focused on career exploration, planning and development, and why the career center can't make their son or daughter come to the career center to explore careers or build a job search strategy.

I did this because parents assume the college is going to do everything in their power to help their sons or daughters prepare for a successful careers within their degrees. But as you know, if you can't get a student to your career center, there is little you can do to help!

My goal was to get parents to understand this so they could play a role in requiring their sons or daughters to take ownership of their careers and use the career center resources from the time they get to campus.

One of the reasons students are not focused on careers is that the administration and culture of the campus is focused everywhere but on careers!

Here are a couple of examples:

MANY colleges require students to invest time in various volunteer activities prior to graduation. It's not unusual for a college to require students to show proof of investing 30-60 hours in volunteering activities in order to graduate. Yet, at the same time, these same institutions do not require students to invest ANY time in career planning and management.

Campus Compact

During my research, I came across an organization called Campus Compact whose focus is to act as a clearing house and support structure for campuses that are committed to require their students to invest a specific amount of time in volunteer and community service projects. Over 1,200 college presidents have signed the Campus Compact which shows their commitment and that of their college to encourage students to adopt civic minded projects and behavior.

In fact in their 2011 yearly report entitled Deepening the Roots of Civic Engagement, they reported that 91% of Campus Compact member schools indicated that their institutions had a mission statement that included service, service-learning, or civic engagement; 90% noted that their strategic plan explicitly addressed these areas. Here is a statement from their website:

Campuses offer a variety of mechanisms for community members to have a voice in campus decision making. Most (78%) offer formal opportunities for community members to discuss concerns with the administration. Nearly three-quarters (74%) include community members on the Board of Trustees. Community members may also serve on committees overseeing academic (29%), hiring (26%), or budgetary (12%) matters.

In the book, I outlined nearly 20 different things colleges are doing to provide students an outlet to learn how and why they should give back to the community. The list of achievements, and more importantly, the time and commitment of students from these 1200 member campuses is impressive. In fact, in 2011, the estimated value of the volunteer time and services provides by students were estimated to exceed $9.1 BILLION dollars.

President's commitment to sustainability

In doing research for a recent blog article titled Annual Mentoring Campaigns, I came across a college that was a member of a national organization that supports sustainability issues on campus. It's called the American College and University President Climate Commitment. This organization has 665 college/university presidents who have signed a commitment to lead and encourage their colleges to take an active part in minimizing their carbon footprint and to educate others about the long term affects our current energy use and policy will have on our planet and culture.

Here is a brief statement the organization's mission:

We believe colleges and universities must exercise leadership in their communities and throughout society by modeling ways to minimize global warming emissions, and by providing the knowledge and the educated graduates to achieve climate neutrality.

So what is my point?

I'm beginning to believe there are a lot more organizations like these that your president and the college are committed to. At the end of the day, I support these, but what I am saddened by is that leadership is committing not only their college, its people, and culture with a stroke of a pen, to require students, faculty and staff to these initiatives, but they are also making a financial investment. In tough economic times, your college is going to have to start to identify which organizations match their principal missions and core competences.

What we should all be concerned about is that these memberships and organizations are taking away from your need to keep students focused on taking ownership of their careers from the time they arrive on campus.

Do yourself a favor!

Have someone on your team begin to inventory the number of groups and organizations your college is committed to and try to evaluate the amount of time and commitment students, staff, and faculty are required to invest in them. Then use that information to bring light to the fact that it's time the college begin to focus more on career planning and development on campus.

IT TAKES A CAMPUS TO BUILD A SUCCESSFUL CAREER!

Virtual village of volunteer career support increases retention,
graduation rate, and payback of college loans!

Some people say, Hillary Clinton's 1994 book, It Takes a Village, got its name from an African proverb; "It takes a village to raise a child."

Hillary reminds us that while parents are THE most important influence on raising a child, the village around that child is also responsible for imbuing ethics, leadership, citizenship and a moral standard to support the community.

Today, I wanted to explore how important it is for college students to have a "village" of support to help guide, mentor and advise them on how they can translate all they are learning into strategies to build successful careers.

In reading a New York Times article by Jason DeParle, called For Poor, Leap to College Often Ends in a Hard Fall, I realized how incredibly important a support group is to a college student. Jason shares the realities low income, high achieving students face when trying to develop enough velocity to escape the issues, relationships and economics that define who they are the minute they leave home for college.

He follows three Galveston Texas girls who shared a desire to "get off the island" and make something of themselves. As the story unfolds, the realities of having to work part time to pay for college, the pull of boyfriends "on the island" with fewer ambitions, and depression caused by the sheer force required to break away from a life that, like gravity continues to ground their dreams and aspirations of finishing college are constant influences.

And this story does not have a happy ending.

Not only do the girls commit years to attempt to get college degrees, but in the case of Angelica Gonzales, end up working for $9.50 per hour after spending over $200,000 on an education! The horribly sad part of this story is that there are millions of students from wealthy, middle class, and struggling class families who are living similar stories. Each want their part of the American dream that starts with a college degree which should qualify them for the next level of opportunities to join generations before them that enjoyed gaining access to a middle class life complete with healthcare, cars, homes and occasional vacations, while at the same time saving for retirement.

The article discussed a series of missed opportunities in helping the girls graduate. Some were caused by cultural issues, others by the stress they were under, and yet others were caused by the lack of having a support group to help them through the issues.

The colleges the girls chose had counselors, but these counselors did not have the bandwidth to keep following up with the girls, coach them, give them pep talks and steer them in the right directions when the undertow from their realities increased.

When you think about it, it's shocking that our "village" condones a system that gives students like Angelica Gonzales a glimpse at a dream that will change their lives, but after decades of seeing the system is broken, does not offer the support, guidance, and help needed to keep the dream alive.

The system we have in place today results in <u>nearly 60% of students entering college who end up with college debt, no degree and in a worse situation</u> then they were in before they entered college.

Doesn't higher education, AND the community have a responsibility to right this situation?

So that got me thinking...

What kind of support group would any student, but even more importantly, a low-income student need? I started jotting down a list of possible "village" positions that could be marshaled to help students and their parents who are investing the cost of an average home to earn a degree.

Imagine if every incoming freshman had a support group consisting of:

1) Career counselors

Colleges already have a team of career counselors that are stretched in serving the population base their administration assigns them. With the average career counselor responsible for over 1,600 students, it's nearly impossible to provide strategic advice. In my perfect world, colleges would reduce that number to 400 and students would be required to visit either in person or by phone with their career counselors.

2) Career coaches

The neat thing about us humans is that we are all different. Each of us has strengths, skills, capacity for knowledge, and passions. While a college career counselor in the career center might be adequate for some students, a full time/dedicated career coach may be needed for others. Career coaches can work on a monthly basis to keep students focused on a methodology and career plan designed to help them build a successful career strategy.

3) Alumni mentors

One of the most underutilized areas that all colleges could be drawing on is alumni. With 50 to 100 plus years of graduates, every college has a collection of willing alumni who under the right circumstances would be willing to provide guidance and help to students and grads.

4) Community mentors

Every day 10,000 boomers with skills, knowledge, experience, contacts and expertise in a variety of areas are retiring. This group has time and resources, with many looking for a way to give back, provide some relevance to their new found free time, and help others.

5) Company/Organization mentors

Businesses and organizations have an opportunity --and more today than ever-- have a desire to engage with students early on in their college experience so they have an opportunity to help guide and help students understand what they will need to do to successfully migrate from college to the corporate life.

6) Parents

It also got me thinking about what role parents could/should play in this process as well as what kind of support, knowledge and training THEY need to do their part in helping their sons or daughters stay focused on the end game, graduation and a job!

One solution that TalentMarks has been introducing is a CareerParent online community that delivers career videos, webinars, discussions and resources that help parents understand why their sons or daughters need to take ownership of their careers from the time they come to campus.

But we already have these!

I know you are going to say you already have some or all of these opportunities... but at what scale? And does your college REALLY focus on them? In order to decrease the dropout rate, and help more students graduate on time, we are going to have to put more resources into a support structure and make it a part of the college culture!

What if you could assign to every incoming freshman a "virtual volunteer career support village"? What if you could use technology to track the students' progress as well as keep the team working together to help, nudge, nurture, advise and guide the student through the steps they will need to take in order to graduate with a job?

Could this support group help increase the retention rate-- the number of grads that not only graduate-- but graduate with jobs?

I think so!

UNIVERSITY OF PHOENIX BUILDS COLLEGE CULTURE AROUND CAREER EXPLORATION & MANAGEMENT

A revolutionary new career services model will have all 4,000 colleges in the United States, if not all 14,000 colleges worldwide, scrambling to catch up!

University of Phoenix®

In my book, The Unemployed Grad, And What Parents Can Do About It, I examined why the culture on college campuses does not focus on careers. My goal was to help parents understand how dramatically the job search process has changed and what they could do to coach their students to take ownership of their careers from the time they get on campus, so that they don't run the risk of becoming part of the 53.6% of grads under 25 that are either unemployed or underemployed identified in last year's Associated Press study.

I wasn't surprised then, when a survey of 600 career directors late last year, conducted by NACE for the Career Advisory Board showed:

- 48.1% thought students did not have the knowledge they needed to find a job.

- 55.7% felt students' resumes were not professional enough to use for their job searches.

The survey confirmed the pleas I heard in conversations with hundreds of career professionals about the need for colleges to change their cultures to focus on careers to better prepare graduates for the workforce.

University of Phoenix gets this

One college that has rapidly transformed its culture to focus on education that leads to careers and helping their students and alumni find the right careers, as well as providing the right courses that match employers' needs, is the University of Phoenix. It's newly launched ***Phoenix Career Services*** is a win-win solution designed to help channel prospective and current students to the career paths that best match their interests so they can better position themselves for the open positions that are the right fit for them among the more than 3 million jobs that are available in the U.S.

The University's transformation is somewhat akin to what Microsoft did when Bill Gates, then CEO, issued a now famous December 7th, 1995 "Internet Tidal Wave" memo that suggested the Internet was going to become the central focus of their products and services, and he urged employees to immediately begin to think how every product and service could be adapted, modified and or delivered by the Internet. Industry experts doubted that Gates could "turn their ship around" and refocus their product development and delivery via the Internet. History proved he could and did!

University of Phoenix is transforming their culture by focusing on two things: students and the companies that hire them.

Focus on students

University of Phoenix decided to put an assessment at the very beginning, prior to the enrollment process, so potential students have a better idea of which career paths they should take. They wanted to help students better identify their career paths before they even applied, so they could then explore possible degree programs and even job postings.

To do this, University of Phoenix created a free, five-minute online assessment tool that is available 24/7 to anyone who wants to use it. Career Interest Profiler helps people identify their professional interests and the related careers to better focus their career search. It's a valuable tool for anyone considering going to college because it rapidly helps them identify the kind of careers where they will more likely be the happiest and find most success, before they even consider applying to the college.

Career Interest Profiler is interactive and is something a prospective student can explore as much as he or she wants. While the assessment tool might take only 5 minutes, it's easy to see anyone could spend much, much longer interacting and engaging with the suggestions and data provided. Frankly, it's the first scalable solution I've seen that will give prospective students the knowledge and information they need to identify what they want to do in their careers.

More importantly, it helps them see the types of careers that match their interests, and displays degree programs that University of Phoenix offers that will help them qualify for the right jobs. This tool alone could help prevent students going down career paths that aren't right for them.

Next, University of Phoenix developed the free Job Market Research Tool to help people identify the education, experience and skills typically required of the jobs and career paths they are interested in, as well as typical salary ranges for those careers. Anyone using this tool can drill down deeper and see companies that are doing the most hiring and learn more about specific skills required for the jobs. For example, if I wanted a marketing manager position, I could see which companies are hiring, and what specialized skills, software skills and basic skills I would need for the job. Plus, I could see the type of career paths individuals have taken moving into and out of those positions.

Armed with the data developed from the person who takes the Career Interest Profiler, the Job Market Research Tool allows potential students to visually see a common career path (from actual data) of successful job candidates. In my marketing example above, I could see the 5 most common types of positions Marketing Managers had prior to getting the position, AND I can see the 5 most common types of positions they had after their Marketing Manager positions ended.

This process gives prospective students more confidence in the fact that the path they are choosing is not only one that best fits their interests and passions, but by analyzing recent job postings, it gives them a better idea of employment options and market demand for their chosen careers.

Finally, for students who choose to pursue an education with the University, Phoenix Career Services offers My Career Plan – a personalized education roadmap that allows students to create their own customized plans for developing the competencies that match the needs of their desired careers. The career plan helps students realize where their coursework directly ties to their careers. Students are also required to take additional assessments to determine strengths and areas to develop including additional skills like teamwork and problem solving that employers demand, as well as participate in activities tied directly to the job hunt such as resume writing, building an online presence, and interviewing skills.

From the moment students visit phoenix.edu to take the career assessment on through to graduation, this new career services model is preparing University of Phoenix students to educate themselves about their career paths and, most importantly, what employers are seeking most in new hires.

Focus on companies

Companies have been grumbling for decades that students are not prepared for their first professional jobs. They've identified a dozen or so soft skills students don't have, complain that they have to provide expensive orientation and training programs and lament when, after making that investment, the new hire leaves within 24 months. Yet no one has listened to them... Until now...

University of Phoenix has been actively meeting with and developing relationships with hiring authorities at top employers across the country. They continue to ask employers what they need from their employees and are taking that information into consideration when developing their curricula and academic programs.

Focus on the customers' needs!

Most businesses fail because they don't focus on their customers' needs. University of Phoenix has put additional time and effort into build their culture around the needs of their students, alumni and the companies that hire them, and I expect this strategy will benefit all areas.

How?

By building a culture that is focused on outcomes, University of Phoenix is helping more grads find the right careers, which may help reduce hiring costs for companies by providing more qualified candidates. That's a big payoff!

4

WHO ARE YOUR CUSTOMERS? STUDENTS OR THE COMPANIES THAT HIRE THEM?

In a previous article we talked about the need to listen to what your students and grads want from your department.

I wanted you to evaluate your services, curriculum and products to determine if they were relevant to your students' needs. In the process we wanted you to question if the programs, policies and strategies that your career center had were designed for the career center's or the college's benefit or your students' benefits.

Instead of putting your student in the customer seat, today, I'd like you to think about putting the businesses and organizations that hire your students in the customers' seats.

It's a thought that the University of Phoenix is not only considering, but implementing. Recently I spoke with Mr. Mike Mayor, the SVP of Education to Careers at the University of Phoenix. Mike was challenged by his board and management to completely restructure and redefine career services to make it more relevant to both the firms that hire students as well as the students themselves, none of whom have been able to keep pace with the dramatic changes that are occurring in the job search process.

According to Mike Mayor,

"It's unsettling for most people to think of a university as a factory but that's exactly what it is. Universities take in raw material, shape it, mold it, and (hopefully) enhance it according to buyers' specifications. To say our student is the customer is like saying an unfinished car on the assembly line is Ford's customer."

His entrepreneurial background gave Phoenix an opportunity to introduce new approaches and ideas and not be bound by decades old mantras and dogma. Mike recognized that the way companies typically engage and work with universities focuses on what the colleges want. Colleges are interested in getting the company to send their employees back to college to pick up the skills to lead the company, and offer their employees tuition assistance.

Yet businesses feel that if the people they hire have the right talent and skills, they won't have to send employees through basic skills and knowledge courses.

So back in 2010, Mike helped to create the strategy behind Workforce Solutions – a 500-strong field force from the University of Phoenix designed to listen to employers needs' and focus on giving those employers the right talent faster and with less cost. Today, their crew has developed nearly 2,000 business partnerships that are designed around the needs of the businesses and organizations that hire graduates.

To further show their commitment to employers and employees, the University of Phoenix wanted to find a way to reduce the hassle of the job search process.

Their goal was to adopt emerging social media and take advantage of the changing behaviors of consumers and companies to help their students not only find jobs, but be found by employers. So they developed a technology that takes a "cue" from dating sites. In this program, both employers and job seekers will be able to identify what criteria they are looking for and the program instantly produces a list of opportunities.

For the job seeker, the program will only show jobs for which they will qualify. Hiring managers will be able to set the criteria they are looking for and dial down, or up, the criteria based on the list of job seekers they are presented. This program is dynamically changed by both the hiring manager and the prospective employee. It's a great way to cut through the clutter for both because it provides more relevant matches.

For employers this process will save time, deliver the right kind of employees with the skill sets they need and cut the hiring cost. For job seekers, the system will increase the likelihood they will find a job that matches their skills, interests, behaviors and personalities, resulting in a more satisfying, rewarding and successful career.

For both, it offers an opportunity to increase retention and job stability.

WHAT ARE YOUR PLANS TO INCREASE THE NUMBER OF CAREER CENTER VISITS?

Presented by DeVry University

I've been pouring over the study by the Career Advisory Board, called Effectively Counseling Graduating Students. The CAB engaged NACE to survey career center professionals to find out if graduating students are prepared to enter the job market and succeed in their first jobs.

The survey was shared with 1,365 career professionals and a whopping 43 percent, or nearly 600, participated.

The results showed that career professionals do NOT think grads are job search ready. In fact:

- 8.0 percent strongly disagree

- 40.1 percent disagree

- 27.7 percent neither agree nor disagree

- 21.6 strongly agree

- 2.7 agree

I'm not sure why 27.7 percent neither agreed or disagreed. Perhaps it was because they just didn't know, or that they didn't want to weigh in on the topic. Rather than focusing on the negative number, let's focus on the positive. If we can extrapolate this survey to career center professionals across the country, only 23 percent think their graduating seniors are ready for their job searches.

Frankly I'm not surprised.

In a 2011 survey conducted by NACE that evaluated how frequently graduating seniors visited the career center:

- 27 percent never visited

- 18.1 percent visited once

- 16.7 percent visited twice.

That adds up to nearly 60 percent who either never visit or visit less than twice. Clearly that is not enough time to even prepare a resume.

So what is the solution?

- 33.7 percent suggest offering, requiring students to attend career classes

- 18.3 percent suggest cultivating relationships with faculty

- 11.9 percent suggested moving the career center to a more visible location

- 7.7 percent suggested hiring paid student ambassadors

- 16.6 percent suggested mores staff to market the career center to students

We'd like to suggest a couple of our solutions too.

1. Our CareerWebinar series will get students thinking about their careers and visiting the career center

2. Our CareerParent program will get parents to encourage their sons or daughters to visit the career center

3. Our CareerFair program will increase student contact with the companies that hire students and encourage them to visit the career center

4. Our CareerChat will take inquiries from students and encourage them to visit the career center Our CareerCourses will deliver the courses survey participants overwhelmingly recommended students take, at any time, through any device.

I'd like to suggest a couple of TalentMarks solutions too.

1. CareerWebinar series will get students thinking about their careers and visiting the career center
2. CareerParent program will get parents to encourage their sons or daughters to visit the career center
3. CareerChat will take inquiries from students and encourage them to visit the career center
4. CareerCourses will deliver the courses survey participants overwhelmingly recommended students take, at any time, through any device.

The CAB report clearly supports what Martin Yate said in the preface. The current career services model is broken and it's time to implement the solutions that will help more students get internships and grads land jobs!

6

IN GRADS' TIME OF NEED, COLLEGES CUT CAREER CENTER BUDGETS

Is your college doing enough to help your graduates get jobs? <u>Tens of thousands of parents and business professionals don't think you are.</u>

Why?

If you are like most colleges your management has imposed budget cuts, or at best, budget freezes on the career center, at a time when:

1. The number of grads who had jobs by graduation day plummeted from over 50% in 2007 to approximately 20% since 2008.

2. The time it takes a grad to get a job now takes an excruciating 7.4 months, and of those grads 60% will be working in jobs unrelated to their majors.

3. Alumni unemployment has doubled.

4. Techniques to look for a job have dramatically changed due to the rapid upswing by hiring managers to use Social Media channels and new Internet tools.

5. What the average student owes continues to rise, with the average student owing over $25,000 in student loan debt, and nearly $5,000 in credit card debt.

Think for a moment. With all of these changes in the past 4 years, what is your career center doing differently to help grads and alumni?

If you college is like most, management's spending priorities are sending a strong signal to prospective parents and grads that your college is more interested in getting them to enroll than helping them prepare for their careers. Looking for proof?

- The latest National Association of Colleges and Employers research shows the average career center has had to make nearly 4% in budget cuts the past two years.

- The 2011 State of College Admissions" report compiled by the National Association of College Admission Counseling found that the average private college will spend over $3,042.52 to recruit an enrolled student (a 56% increase over 2007).

- The report mentioned above suggests that a college with 400 grads is only spending $84 per grad to prepare them for their careers.

This lack of investment shows because <u>surveys clearly identify that grads don't have a clue about how to search for jobs.</u>

- 60 percent of grads spend only 1-5 hours a week on their job searches

- 61 percent of grads had only 1 alumni mentor each

- 95 percent do not have a job search plans

When your grads don't get jobs by graduation day, they are not only losing $3,000 to $4,000 each month, <u>but your college will end up getting blamed by students, government, parents, journalists and businesses.</u>

You could have a mammoth effect on your grads' careers if you reinvested in your career center. If your investment helped just one student get a job 4 months faster than the national average indicates, it's like giving them a $12,000 to $16,000 graduation present! Imagine helping 10 or even 100!

You have a choice!

Ignore this opportunity and I guarantee this situation will dramatically affect recruitment and future contributions. By reinvesting in your career center, you could put yourself ahead of competitors, and better serve grads and alumni at the same time.

We've outlined 12 ways you could accomplish this in our new report, "Create a Career Centered College Culture and Campus". Hillary Clinton suggested that, "It takes a village to educate a student." On a college campus, you will need the support and engagement of faculty, staff, and administrators to build a curriculum on your campus that supports your career center's objectives and goals.

Hundreds of business professionals and career center staff have endorsed these steps as necessary in order to better prepare graduates for the limited opportunities available.

You would be wise to explore the options this report offers as this is not an issue you can ignore any longer.

A perfect storm is brewing that is being fueled by government regulations, parent and grad dissatisfaction, competition from cheaper college education alternatives, modifications in student loans, changes in state and federal funding, and business organizations. If you want to stay ahead of the changes these organizations want, you need to start planning today.

Failure to explore these ideas will result in your competitors leap frogging you--something you cannot afford to let happen.

REQUIRE - MAKE - DEMAND STUDENTS INVEST TIME IN THEIR CAREERS

Did you realize that 71% of graduates wished they had done something differently while in college to prepare them for the job market?

Two studies, one by Adecco, and the other by the John J. Heldrich Center for Workforce Developments, found that grads regret not spending more time looking for jobs, networking and developing career plans while in college.

In the Adecco 2011 "College Graduate Survey":

- 26 percent wished they started their job search earlier

- 29 percent wished they had networked more

- 26 percent wished they had applied for more jobs prior to graduation

- And, in the Heldrich 2012 report entitled Chasing the American Dream:

- 37 percent would have been more careful at selecting a major

- 29 percent would have done more to work part time or get an internship

- 20 percent would have taken classes to prepare for a career

Let me remind you again about the NACE survey that found that over 61 percent of seniors never went to the career center, or visited once, or maximum twice.

What plans do you have to help current students not become more statistics and also regret never visiting the career center? By doing nothing, your college is positioning another graduation class for a stunted, disappointing career start.

In my mind, all you would have to do is show these two reports to management to prove that you need to implement some kind of program that requires, or at minimum STRONGLY recommends that students invest time in developing career plans.

The career center is just another club on campus!

We like to remind parents that the career center is simply a campus club. It's one of hundreds of organizations in which their students can participate. Unfortunately, few students take advantage of their services.

The only way this can be changed is if management at colleges changes the culture on campus and raise the awareness of and the importance of the career center. In a rather exhaustive report, Create a Career Centered College Culture and Curriculum, TalentMarks offers 12 ways your management can accomplish that.

The Career Advisory Board survey found that students have a poor understanding of how to properly conduct successful job searches and also lack some of the tools and skills necessary to locate and acquire jobs. Over 77 percent of the 593 career directors that completed the survey felt that the greatest obstacle to be overcome in counseling students wishing to enter the job market was getting students to understand the effort required to conduct those job searches.

But how can you get students to take ownership of their careers?

The survey offered these suggestions from career directors:

- 44.9% thought students should be required to take career course.

- 18.3% thought a better working relationship with faculty would help.

- 16.6% identified hiring more staff to be critical to increase student career preparedness.

- 11.9% felt that moving the career center to a higher trafficked area could increase awareness.

- 7.6% identified hiring student ambassadors to promote career management as beneficial.

- 0.9% thought gaining 3rd party expertise could help.

The number one suggestion will be difficult to implement. The staff will have to first write a proposal for management and present their idea. Management will ask them to conduct a study that will include surveying students and faculty and analyzing competitors and industry best practices, identifying what should be included in the curriculum, who will teach it, and how it will fit into the students' schedules. <u>At this point, a year will have gone by</u>. Then, it will take another 3 months to get on management's schedule to do a presentation, at which time management will provide limited funds to begin to develop the curriculum. Assuming this is going to be done by existing staff, who also have to fit it into their schedules, another year goes by! You get the picture? Just to bring a career course to market could take 2-3 years and an enormous amount of time and effort!

I'd like to see the President's cabinet pick this up as a priority.

You may not be aware of this but over 1200 college presidents have signed the Campus Compact, which commits their institution to the tenets of the Campus Compact which requires students to fulfill a minimum number of hours in community service or volunteer opportunities in order to graduate.

In order to support this pledge, colleges have invested in full time staff that have developed a variety of events and activities and have built relationships with community organizations and programs to give their students the channels they need to fulfill their part of the charter.

In my research, I've <u>been unable to find a similar organization that encourages colleges to require students to take ownership of their careers</u>.

Yet an annual American freshman poll conducted by UCLA shows the primary reason students are going to college is to get a job, NOT to learn how to be a volunteer! In fact 85.9% of first-year students across the country said that being able to land a good job is a very important reason for attending college. That is the strongest response to that question in the 40 years it has been asked and is sharply higher than the 70.4% reply in 2006, before the recession began.

This should be sending a strong signal to college campuses around the country to require students to commit a minimum number of hours prior to graduation, so that career exploration, developing career plans and picking up job search skills are touted more often.

Studies and research we are sharing in this report also suggest that students and parents are expecting their college careers will result in jobs which will in turn result in ample money to pay back loans and enable grads to settle into the American dream and buy things like cars and houses, and even take vacations.

NACE studies also clearly demonstrate that students who use their career centers more frequently not only get internships, but they get jobs faster and at higher rates. The challenge colleges have is to develop a formula that will require students to take ownership of their careers. We don't see colleges adopting required curriculums in the next 5 years. However, within the decade it could become more prevalent. In the meantime, it will be incumbent on the colleges to come up with strategies that will encourage students to take ownership of their careers.

So what can you do to increase career ownership?

1. Engage parents and educate them as to why they should require their sons or daughters to begin building career plans from the beginning of their campus experiences.

2. Ramp up marketing efforts to students to make them aware of the research that shows the more they invest, the better chance that they will get jobs at higher pay.

3. Continue reading this book!

4. Adopt social media marketing strategies and design systems so that anything a student does to develop his or her career plan can be shared through a social network.

5. Adopt badge technology to give electronic "pats on the back" and public recognition for working on and managing career strategies.

6. Provide a "certification" program that provides students proof they have completed a career development and management curriculums.

7. Encourage business leaders to require students to share their certifications.

You are working at a great time to make significant contributions and bring powerful changes that will help prepare students for their first professional job searches and give them foundations to lead to successful careers. Start discussions on campus to create a college that is focused on careers.

"When we leverage, we aggregate and organize existing resources to achieve success."

— Richie Norton
The Power of Starting Something Stupid

IT ALL STARTS WITH RESOURCES

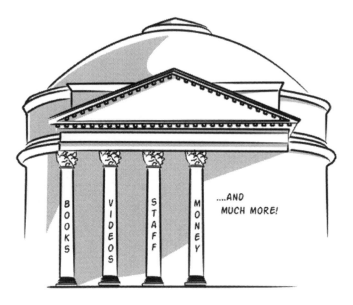

Have we covered enough material for you yet!

My goal has been to inspire and ignite your passions so you become a tireless, fearless and LOUD advocate of fundamentally transitioning the culture on campus from one that is focused on athletics, events and activities to one that is founded on careers.

And, as we have talked at length, you can't do it alone.

Nor can you do it without the right resources and staffing. So let's venture off in conclusion to talk about how to get the right resources to make your vision, strategy and plan work.

It all starts here!

10 WAYS TO GET MORE RESOURCES FOR YOUR CAREER CENTER

Take an entrepreneurial approach and get the budget you need to

prepare graduates for a lousy job market!

A lot has changed in the employment world since 2007.

In 2007, nearly 60% of the students graduating had jobs by graduation day. Another 12% -19% went on to advanced degrees, which left a little over 20% without jobs. In hindsight, these were the good old days!

Today, on a nationwide basis, things have flipped. Only 20% of the students graduating from college have a job and 80% are unemployed. It's a miserable time for graduates to be stepping into the cold, cruel world, particularly when you combine the fact that they are leaving college with the highest credit card and student loan debt of any students in the history of our country, or in fact, the world.

On top of that, the employment world has flipped too!

Prior to 2007, while online job boards were emerging, the primary way to find a job was simply looking through classified ads in various publications.

Today's students have to be adept at using online search techniques and social media and master the skills involved in creating a resume that will be picked up due to their focus on the right keywords, networking skills and understandings about how to build job search strategies.

Having a good resume is only one of a half a dozen (or more) skills they will need to stand out in an uncertain job market. For the graduates of 2007 and prior, having their degrees and good resumes were all they needed to get out and get interviews. Interviews and job offers came easily and most students didn't prepare-- in fact, 'winging it" was common.

Unfortunately, today's students, grads and alumni need more training, and more services, and college management is freezing or cutting the budgets of career centers. We've held a series of "virtual town hall meetings" to learn more about what career centers needed which led to a Webinar and white paper that outlined 10 Ways To Get *More* Resources for Your Career center.

The top ten strategies that came out of our discussions and research included:

1. Using stats to show a need

2. Starting a discussion comparing your piece of the pie

3. Showing you can improve retention

4. Showing you can help recruiting

5. Developing a student 4-year plan

6. Identifying how you can deliver services more cost effectively

7. Rebranding yourself

8. Generating your own revenue

9. Reaching out to volunteers

10. Identifying the "Cadillac" example

If you are interested in more details, visit www.talentmarks.com, click on consulting and download the white paper and listen to a recorded webinar focusing on the topic.

"Thrift means that you should always have the best you can possibly afford, when the thing has any reference to your physical and mental health, to your growth in efficiency and power."

-Orison Swett Marden

12

PENNYWISE AND POUND FOOLISH?

Are colleges and universities allocating resources to the departments that will make the most impact on college students' careers?

While the college continues its mission to provide students a rigorous curriculum that qualifies them for their degrees, the career center has traditionally been under-funded and more recently has been asked to do more, with less.

In fact, the 2011 NACE Research report shows the median budget spiraling down when--as the previous points suggest --more resources should be provided. Their report indicates career centers had to cut their budgets by:

• 2.9 percent in 2010/2011 school year

• 1.5 percent in 2009/2010 school year

According to the report the average median budget fell to only $33,000 per year and the 2012 report showed the average median budget dropped even LOWER to $31,000.

Now keep in mind this is for non-personel costs. It covers the cost for conferences, software, books, speakers, and money that goes for resources to help the career center build career and job search strategies.

Let's look at that budget from a different perspective. Let's examine it from a budget-per-student based on different sized colleges. Based on a budget of $31,000 per year for the career center:

- A small college with 1,200 students would be investing $25.83 per student.

- A slightly larger college with 2,500 students would be investing $12.40 per student.

- A medium sized college of 5,000 student would be $6.20 per student.

These costs are in career tools such as assessments, books, and speakers, and in miscellaneous services and advice.

So, depending on the size of the college, management is suggesting $6.20 to $25.83 is a worthy amount to help prepare graduates for their careers.

What do you think?

We don't think those figures come to enough. In my white paper, *10 Ways to Get More Resources For Your Career Center,* we suggested that you compare your per-student budget to the budgets of orientation, student affairs, athletics, transportation and even admissions.

Let's put this into perspective and look at what is being spent in other departments per student.

Admissions cost per enrolled student

In 2007, Lipman Hearne released a study on marketing expenditures of 157 institutions ranging from research institutions to small liberal arts colleges. The report, *Key Insights April 2007*, revealed that spending within college and university marketing and communications programs increased 50 percent between 2000 and 2007.

Industry experts affirmed the logic of increased admissions marketing budgets:

Rae Goldsmith, then vice president for communications and marketing at CASE, said of the study, *"What this survey points out is that the more an institution invests in strategic marketing and communications, the more it will gain in terms of achieving student recruitment and other goals."*

Wow! Wouldn't you love to hear someone in a leadership position at your college make that statement for your career center? Let's see how that sounds:

<Your college president's name here> says *"What we have determined is that the more we invest in helping the students and alumni build successful careers, the faster they transition from unemployed to gainful employment, the higher the salaries they get and the more contributions we receive over time!"*

The Lipman Hearne report showed that the average four-year private institution spent about $1,941 to recruit a student, and the average four-year public institution spent about 20 percent of that amount ($398).

That was then. Today it's significantly higher!

The National Association of College Admission Counseling 2011 *State of College Admissions* report shows the average:

• Private colleges spent $3,042.52 to recruit an enrolled student

• State colleges spent $987.01 to recruit an enrolled student

Now compare that to the career student budget per student that ranged from $6.60 to $27.50! Budgets to recruit students are continuing to rise and yet the budgets to help students matriculate into their careers continue to fall, requiring career professionals to do more with less.

Does that seem fair for career professionals and students? Does it show where college priorities are?

Now let's look at staffing

Colleges have anywhere from 150 to 2,000 faculty teaching on their campuses. At many colleges, it's not unusual for a student-to-faculty ratio of 1 faculty person to 20 students. Soka University in Orange County claims a 1-to-9 ratio. Wow!

Career center professionals could only dream of providing that level of individual coaching and level of commitment and service to students.

The same NACE Research report mentioned above also reported that:

- The average ratio of students to full-time professional career staff was calculated to be 2,890 students per FTE staff member (1 to 2,890).

- The average ratio of students per career counselor is 9,377 students per counselor (1 to 9,377).

- The average number of counseling appointments per career counselor is 1,863 per year.

You do the math.

If a career counselor dedicated even ½ of the 2,000 hours they work each year to career coaching, the effects will be negligible. The typical college student receives (by our estimates) less than 4 hours of career advisement and coaching in the four years of their college career - when they should have 10 times that.

The National Association of College Admissions Officers 2011 *State of College Admission Counseling* report suggests that the admissions office is significantly better staffed than the career center.

Their surveys found that on average the ratio of applicants to admission officers at colleges and universities in the US was:

- 1 to 981 at public institutions

- 1 to 402 at private institutions

I always felt a bit of empathy for admissions officers who had to deal with a huge influx of applications during their "season" <u>but compared to what career center staff and career center counselors have to deal with year round-- well, there is no comparison; career centers have a much greater workload.</u>

The career center staff clearly wins the contest of being the leanest group on campus.

But should they be?

Is this the message you want to send to your prospective students and parents? What do you think your prospective students and parents will think of your career advisor to student counseling ratio? Is it a number you share or hide?

In today's competitive times, we think it's a number you should share, as long as you invest in more career advisors.

SUMMARY

We realize these are difficult times for colleges and universities.

Presidents and upper management would be wise to evaluate travel and conference, salaries, and take a hard look at all departments on campus to find ways to deliver more resources to the career center. Every department and every resource should be evaluated for its contribution to the end game for graduates – to help them have successful careers!

Nicholas Negroponte, founder and chairman of One Laptop per Child, suggests that perspective is worth 50 IQ points. He suggests that organizations would be wise to consider from what perspective they are attempting to solve these problems that students face today. If colleges and universities look at this from the traditional angle which is from inside the organization and/or industry, they may very likely be trying to solve an institutional problem and not the problem students, grads and alumni want solved. As you look at your situation make sure you look at it from your customers' perspective and learn what it is they want you to do for them.

Frankly, the career center's budget is SO LOW already (median $33,000 per school per year according to 2011 NACE Research), it wouldn't take the chief finance officer at the college more than 10 minutes to find areas to shift funds that would QUADRUPLE the career center budget!

If they can't find the money by shifting it out of unproductive areas, the CFOs might take this as an opportunity to look at how they can lower costs by searching outside their industry. A report issued by the National Center for Education Statistics in November of 2011, might give administrators a benchmark they should aim for:

According to the report, on average, for-profit schools spent $2,659 per student on instructional costs during the 2008-09 academic, compared with $9,418 per student at public universities and $15,289 per student at private, non-profit colleges.

Non-profit colleges could learn a couple lessons from their for-profit cousins, not only about how to effectively run online education, but to hold costs down.

These are difficult times for graduates and alumni.

Bold moves need to be taken on campuses to align the costs of education to the emerging competitive opportunities and economic times, yet provide a return on investment for students, grads, alumni and the families and businesses that support them.

Colleges and universities would be wise to invest more in career education, even if they have to reduce services in other departments on campus.

A perfect storm of significantly reduced labor demand, increased foreign competition, and economic and government regulations is making it harder than ever for grads to find work.

ACKNOWLEDGEMENTS

A special thanks to everyone took the time to share advice, brainstorm and kick around ideas on how we can make radical changes in how we prepare students and grads for successful careers.

ABOUT THE AUTHOR

Don Philabaum has a knack for finding a need and solving it.

While in college, Don recognized that graduates wanted a photograph of the symbolic moment the president handed their diploma to them. Colleges could not allow hundreds of parents to approach the stage at the same time, so the moment went undocumented. Acting on his intuition, Don founded a company that developed the technology and marketing process that enabled his team to photograph graduates in a blink of an eye, and then mail a free proof to them. When he sold his firm two decades later, his photographers had captured this once in a lifetime moment for over 3,000,000 graduates and their families.

In 1996, after his online community for college students didn't catch on, (something called Facebook did 8 years later!) Don approached alumni directors whom he worked with in the graduation photography business, and suggested they use his Internet technology to put the alumni directory online. His pioneering firm went on to build 300 alumni online communities for alumni associations in the United States, Europe, and Asia.

Today nearly every student graduating from high school and college is photographed at the moment their diploma is presented to them and, alumni online communities have become a required "tool" in the alumni industry.

Don looks for "Game Changer" opportunities!

So what industry does Don see a great opportunity unfolding? Today, you will find Don focusing on helping college students prepare for their first professional job search, and helping alumni lead successful careers and retirements. To do that, Don's firm TalentMarks is introducing innovative technologies, programs, and methodologies to help colleges create a career centered college culture that supports alumni during the transitions in their careers.

Made in the USA
San Bernardino, CA
30 July 2016